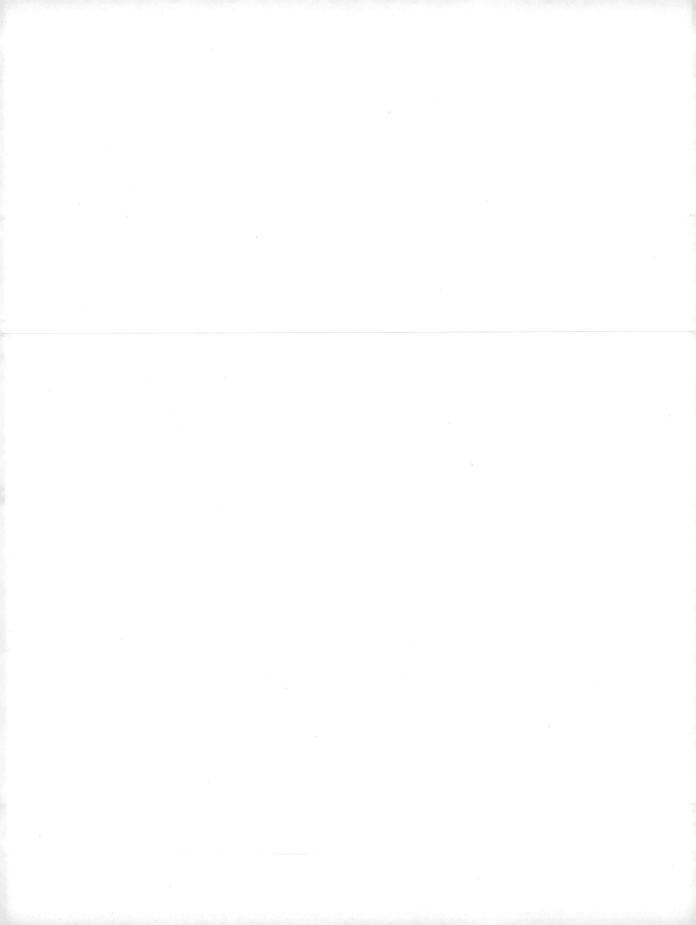

NIGELLA BITES

Also by Nigella Lawson

HOW TO EAT
THE PLEASURES AND PRINCIPLES OF GOOD FOOD

HOW TO BE A DOMESTIC GODDESS
BAKING AND THE ART OF COMFORT COOKING

NIGELLA BITES

FROM FAMILY MEALS TO ELEGANT
DINNERS—EASY, DELECTABLE RECIPES
FOR ANY OCCASION

NIGELLA LAWSON

PHOTOGRAPHY BY FRANCESCA YORKE

NEW YORK

CONTENTS

PREFACE

To tell the truth, I didn't intend to write another book so soon. Not that this is by way of an apology: I am too evangelical about the food I like eating (and cooking) not to want to present the recipes from the new television series, *Nigella Bites,* to you, taking advantage of the extra nattering space a book allows. But I've wanted, too, to borrow from the other medium, so this book is slightly different from my previous two: there are more pictures and the chapters inevitably take their shape and content from each program in the TV series.

In truth, there isn't a conflict. I've always felt that food is nothing if taken out of the context in which it's eaten, and the programs—and consequently these chapters—are arranged according to the sort of cooking we might want to do, depending on our life, our timetable and our mood. But please: these are suggestions only, not inflexible commands. Life is not so rigidly constructed, and I might well want to cook something for a weekday dinner that I've earmarked here for a Sunday lunch, and presume you might, too.

Anyway, even if themes, the focus of these chapters, are varied, what remains constant, and so what links them, is taste. I don't mean taste in a food-snobbish, status sense (please, I am just not interested) but the tendency toward certain techniques (for me, that means easy ones) and certain ingredients. Restaurant chefs rely, to a greater or lesser extent, on innovation and novelty; what's more, they are generally less constrained by ordinary domestic concerns of budget or storage space. They can buy a bottle of some special liqueur for one particular recipe; we are unlikely to. So, you might well find that certain ingredients crop up repeatedly. In the same way, when a little bit of stock is needed, I'm not going to instruct you to start boiling up bones left, right and center, just for the purist sake of it, but rather suggest you use the store-bought broth I use myself. The point is, this is the way we cook at home. And for all that this is, frankly, the book of the television series, I am neither a chef nor a performer: none of the recipes here has been specially constructed for broadcast or publication purposes: this is the food I cook, the food I eat.

At the end of each chapter, I've left a page or two for notes. I wanted to do this for a variety of reasons. It's hardly, in fact, a novel practice: the idea first came to me after riffling through the old, battered books belonging to my grandmothers and my friends' mothers; I found I learned as much from reading their scribbled comments and amendments; it's what made the food come alive for me. Besides, it seemed to me that a book linked to a television series might be used, be read, in a particular way. True, there is slightly more in the book than in the series (where recipes had to be lost because of constraints of broadcast time I've resisted dropping them from the published version), but it seemed to me that while watching the programs, some of you might want to jot things down in the book that accompanies them.

But most of all, this idea came to me out of the

various book signings I've done. Occasionally, people apologize for not coming and buying a new book but rather bringing their own, already stained and dog-eared copies. Believe me, there's no need to apologize: I can't tell you how much this means to me. And the sort of cookbook that's splattered and scribbled over is the only sort of cookbook I want to write. I'm not interested in barking instructions: this isn't meant to be a monologue. As I've said before, I want to be there in the kitchen with you; my words are merely my side of the conversation I imagine we might have. The pages for notes, then, are there for you to make your own response.

NOTE: Eggs, where specified, are large (and preferably organic and free-range); all butter is unsalted, and salmon and meat organic, for preference.

NIGELLA BITES

CHAPTER ONE

ALL-DAY BREAKFAST

While breakfast in the table-laden, leisurely sense might not be an option in our everyday lives, weekends make something a bit more greedy and ceremonial possible. Or just refuse to be constrained by the orthodox timetable and make late-morning breakfast food for whatever time of day you want.

ORANGE BREAKFAST MUFFINS

If you're going to attempt anything other than a bowl of cereal for an ordinary weekday breakfast, then muffins are the best bet. They are the easiest things to make, not least because the laziest of stirring is what's required. The truth is that a heavy, lumpy batter makes for the lightest muffin. Having said that—and this holds true for the recipe that follows, too, of course—no homemade muffin is ever going to be as risen and aeratedly humped as a factory-produced one, nor should it be. The point is a muffin is not a cake. I presume anyway that they were originally devised to be eaten in much the same way as the yeasted version, that's to say as a form of sweet, tender roll with jam. And that's exactly how I eat these. Split them while still warm and, mouthful by mouthful, smear with the best unsalted butter you can find, adding as you want, marmalade, jam or amber, liquid-light honey.

6 tablespoons unsalted butter
1²/₃ cups self-rising flour
2 tablespoons ground almonds
¹/₂ teaspoon baking soda
1 teaspoon baking powder
¹/₄ cup sugar
zest of 1 orange

¹/₃ cup plus 1 tablespoon freshly
 squeezed orange juice
¹/₃ cup plus 1 tablespoon whole milk
1 egg
12-cup muffin pan lined with 12 paper
 baking cups

Preheat the oven to 400°F.

Melt the butter and set aside. Combine the flour, ground almonds, baking soda, baking powder, sugar and orange zest in a large bowl. Measure the orange juice and milk into a pitcher and whisk in the egg and then the cooled, melted butter. Now pour the liquid ingredients into the dry ingredients, mixing with a fork as you go. The batter will be lumpy but that's as it should be: you want everything to be no more than barely combined. The whole point of muffin mixture is that it must never be overworked.

Spoon out the mixture equally into the muffin cups and cook for 20 minutes. Remove, in their paper baking cups, to a wire rack and let cool slightly (but not completely) before devouring.

Makes 12.

WELSH-RAREBIT MUFFINS

I got the idea for these from one of my Amazon-trawled titles, one of those ring-bound American books, called magnificently (and appropriately) *The Joy of Muffins* (by Genevieve Farrow and Diane Dreher). This is my version, and it is great by itself or with a plate of burned and sticky-skinned sausages.

for the muffins:
1½ cups self-rising flour
⅓ cup rye flour
1 teaspoon baking powder
½ teaspoon baking soda
1 teaspoon salt
1 teaspoon English mustard powder
generous ½ cup sharp Cheddar, grated
6 tablespoons vegetable oil
½ cup plus 2 tablespoons plain
   whole-milk yogurt

½ cup whole milk
1 egg
2 tablespoons Worcestershire sauce
12-cup muffin pan lined with 12 paper
   baking cups

for the topping:
2 tablespoons sharp Cheddar, grated
more Worcestershire sauce for sprinkling

Preheat oven to 400°F.

Mix the flours, baking powder, baking soda, salt, mustard powder and cheese in a large bowl with a fork. In a large measuring cup, beat together the remaining ingredients. Pour into the dry ingredients, mixing lightly with your fork, remembering that good muffins are made from lumpy batter.

Pour into the muffin cups and cook for 20 minutes, then quickly take them out of the oven and put a little cheese and a sprinkling of Worcestershire sauce on each one. Put them back in the oven for another 5 minutes, then put the muffins on a baking sheet to cool. Eat them while they are still warm but not hot.

Makes 12.

PANCAKES WITH BACON AND MAPLE SYRUP

While pancakes with syrup are undeniably a supermom-with-kids breakfast cliché, they are also undeniably good, and in my book—which this is, after all—that alone argues forcefully for their inclusion here. They are anyway very easy to make, easier than thinner English pancakes or crêpes, and it's not hard to get into the weekend habit of mixing them up. They're what I make for my children's breakfast on weekends. I make up half quantities of the batter (or the full amount on Saturday, saving half of it in a plastic-wrap-covered container for Sunday) and let them squeeze pancake syrup, rather than the smokier maple, over them; we dispense with the bacon altogether.

Talking of which, if you can, buy pancetta from a deli or a butcher and ask them to slice it finely. This makes for crisp salty wafers, perfect with the resiny sweetness of the syrup. Otherwise ordinary bacon is, of course, fine. It's the fat in the bacon that makes it crisp.

For speed, it makes sense to cook the pancakes in small, dolloped-on rounds, on the griddle or in a nonstick frying pan, but I often use a blini pan, which produces perfect (or as perfect as I am ever going to achieve) 3-inch rounds, as in the picture here. The only drawback is that, unless you dot your stove with blini pans—hardly practical or conducive to early morning cheer—this means cooking them one by one.

2 tablespoons unsalted butter

1 1/2 cups all-purpose flour

2 heaping teaspoons baking powder

1 teaspoon sugar

pinch of salt

1 1/3 cups whole milk

2 eggs

10 slices bacon or approx. 4 ounces wafer-thin-cut pancetta

1–2 teaspoons vegetable oil for frying bacon

butter for frying pancakes

best-quality maple syrup

Melt the butter and set aside to cool slightly while you get on with the rest of the batter and the bacon.

In a large, wide-necked measuring cup, measure out the flour and add the baking powder, sugar and salt. Stir to combine.

In another cup, measure the milk, beat in the eggs and then the slightly cooled butter, and pour the liquid ingredients into the dry ingredients, whisking as you do so. Or just put everything in a blender and blitz.

In the vegetable oil, fry the bacon (cut into half crosswise) or the pancetta strips until crisp, remove to paper towels and cover with more paper towels (not because I'm fat-phobic—as if!—but because this will help them keep their requisite crispness). Now, heat either a griddle or nonstick frying pan, smear with a small bit of butter and then start frying. I just pour small amounts straight from the cup (but you could use a quarter-cup measure if you prefer) so that you have wiggly circumferenced disks about 1¾ inches in diameter. When you see bubbles erupting on the surface, turn the pancakes over and cook for a couple of minutes, if that, on the other side.

Or use a blini pan and, as just described, turn when the bubbles break through to the uncooked surface. There is a Russian saying to the effect that the first pancake is always botched, so be prepared to sacrifice the initial offering to unceremonious stoveside gobbling.

Pile the pancakes onto plates, wigwam with pieces of crispy bacon or pancetta and dribble or pour over, depending on greed and capacity, that clear, brown, woodily fragrant syrup.

Makes about 15 pancakes if cooked in a blini pan; or if not, about 25 pancakes the size of jam-jar lids.

ASIAN-SPICED KEDGEREE

Kedgeree started life, in India, as a dish of lentils and rice and then, translated into the kitchens of what could be called the Anglo-Indian Ascendancy, became an eggy, golden pile of rice punctuated with slabby chunks of smoked haddock. When I was a child it remained as a comforting brunch dish, still part of the homey repertoire of the normal British cook. Here, I've fiddled with it some more, replacing the earthier Indian flavors with the sharper ones of Thailand and Southeast Asia and trading the strident tones of the smoked haddock for gentle, fleshy salmon, beautifully coral against the turmeric-stained gold of the rice. Look for lime leaves at Indian-Pakistani markets or gourmet shops.

2¼ cups cold water for poaching the fish

2 lime leaves, torn into pieces

4 salmon fillets (approx. 1 inch thick), preferably organic, skinned (about 1½ pounds in total)

3 tablespoons unsalted butter

1 teaspoon oil

1 onion, chopped finely

½ teaspoon ground coriander

½ teaspoon ground cumin

½ teaspoon turmeric

1 cup basmati rice

3 hard-boiled eggs, quartered

3 tablespoons chopped cilantro, plus more for sprinkling

juice and zest of a lime plus more lime segments to serve

fish sauce (nam pla) to taste

Preheat the oven to 425°F. This is because the easiest way to poach the salmon for this dish is to do it in the oven. So: pour the water into a roasting pan, add the lime leaves and then the salmon. Cover the pan with foil, put in the oven and cook for about 15 minutes, by which time the salmon should be tender. Remove the pan from the oven and drain the liquid off into a pitcher. Keep the fish warm simply by replacing the foil on the pan.

Melt the butter in a wide, heavy saucepan that has a tight-fitting lid, and add the oil to stop the butter burning. Soften the onion in the pan and add the spices, then keep cooking till the onion is slightly translucent and suffused with the soft perfume of the spices. Add the rice and stir with a wooden spoon so that it's all well coated. There's not enough onion to give a heavy coating: just make sure the rice is fragrantly slicked.

Pour in the reserved liquid from the pitcher—about 2¼ cups—and stir before covering with the lid and cooking gently for about 15 minutes. If your stove is vociferous you may need a flame tamer.

At the end of the cooking time, when the rice is tender and has lost all chalkiness, turn off the heat, remove the lid, cover the pan with a dish towel and then replace the lid. This will help absorb any extra moisture from the rice. It is also the best way to let the rice stand without getting sticky or cold, which is useful when you've got a few friends and a few dishes to keep your eye on.

Just before you want to eat, drain off any extra liquid that's collected in the dish with the salmon, then flake the fish with a fork. Add to it the rice, eggs, cilantro, lime juice and a drop or two of fish sauce. Stir gently to mix—I use a couple of wooden paddles or spatulas—and taste to see if you want any more lime juice or fish sauce. Sprinkle over the zest from the two juiced halves of the lime and serve. I love it served just as it is in the roasting dish, but if you want to, and I often do (consistency is a requirement of a recipe but not a cook), decant into a large plate before you add the lime zest, then surround with lime segments and add the zest and a small handful of freshly chopped cilantro.

This is one of those rare dishes that manages to be comforting and light at the same time. And—should you have leftovers, which I wouldn't count on—it's heavenly eaten, as all leftovers demand to be, standing up, straight from the fridge.

Serves 6.

MASALA OMELETTE

Maybe I should come clean here. Although this is a Keralan dish, I have never, in fact, been to India. But the book's designer had just come back from there when we did the pictures for this book and cooked it for us one day. To eat is to be convinced and the omelette found its way into the TV program. One of the advantages is that it's an unusual thing to eat for breakfast but easy to make, and, what's more, suitable to be cooked for yourself alone. If I'm being honest, I should say that when I cook this for myself, on a weekday at least, I usually dispense with most of the ingredients: I chop two chillies, turn them around in a hot pan with a little bit of oil for a while, then beat them into a couple of eggs, adding some roughly chopped cilantro and Maldon salt at the same time. I then pour everything back into the frying pan and cook for a few minutes before sitting the pan under the grill for a top-setting minute or so.

And feel free to add as well as subtract ingredients: grated ginger is good, as is chopped fresh mint or, indeed, dried. You can eat this flat on the plate, with a knife and fork, or roll it up inside a chapati or another flatbread that you've just warmed through in the microwave.

1 teaspoon vegetable oil	**1 teaspoon ground coriander**
1 scallion, sliced finely	**1 teaspoon ground cumin**
1–2 chillies to taste, red or green	**2 eggs, beaten**
1 clove garlic, finely chopped or grated with a Microplane grater	**freshly chopped cilantro for sprinkling over**
¼ teaspoon turmeric	**chapatis to eat with, if you feel like it**

Preheat the broiler.

Heat the oil in a nonstick frying pan 8 to 10 inches in diameter, and fry the scallion, chilli, garlic and turmeric until soft. Add the other spices and fry for another minute, stirring occasionally, then add the beaten eggs, swirling the pan to help the eggs set underneath.

When the omelette is nearly set, flash it under the hot broiler to finish it off, and serve with chapatis and cilantro or the Green Cilantro Chutney that follows.

Serves 1.

GREEN CILANTRO CHUTNEY

This green and fragrant ointment, for all that it's called a chutney, is perfect, both spiky and, strangely, aromatically cooling with the omelette, to be dolloped on the side of the plate or smeared onto an encircling chapati. I first came across a version of it, some time ago, in Claudia Roden's wonderful book of Jewish food; it's rather poetically a dish of the Jews of India. The main bit of fiddling I've done is to replace the vinegar she stipulates with lime juice. It is deeply gorgeous and takes a minute or so to make. I keep whatever's left over in the refrigerator, but the coconut will harden and thicken there, so remember to take it out to get to room temperature before serving it again. You'll probably need to whiz it up in the processor again, adding a little more lime juice as you do so, too.

The creamed coconut comes in butter-sized slabs and lasts for ages, so you can keep some in a cupboard, on standby. But to be frank, I've never had any difficulty finding it; I even buy it at my local corner shop.

1–5 jalapeño peppers according to taste, seeded and chopped roughly

1-inch piece of ginger, peeled and roughly chopped

4 garlic cloves

⅓ cup creamed coconut or coconut milk, to taste

1 large bunch of cilantro

4 sprigs of mint

½ teaspoon salt

pinch of sugar

the juice of 3 limes

Put the jalapeños, ginger, garlic and creamed coconut into a food processor and blitz to a paste. Add the cilantro and mint and pulse again until the herbs blend. Add the salt and pinch of sugar, then, with the motor running, pour the juice of two and a half limes down the funnel, processing again to mix thoroughly. Taste to see if you want the juice of the remaining half lime.

Put whatever remains into a jar and refrigerate it for up to a month. As I've said, it will solidify, but this is easily corrected by leaving it at room temperature.

BLOODY MARY—A PITCHERFUL

Bloody Mary is the girl for me. A late-morning breakfast, one that oozes into lunch and then into late afternoon, needs liquid accompaniment, and this is what I'd always choose. I steep dried chilli peppers in a bottle of vodka to use just for Bloody Mary, but you don't have to be as extravagantly specialist.

A friend of mine who once worked as a bartender in Hong Kong introduced me to the trick of adding a little dry sherry to the mix, and I gladly pass it on to you now.

1¹/₃ **cups (10 ounces) chilli vodka**
  (or ordinary vodka and a few
  splashes Tabasco)
splash dry sherry
2¹/₂ **cups (20 ounces) tomato juice,**
  chilled

juice of a quarter to half a lemon
  (to taste)
few shakes of celery salt
few dashes Worcestershire sauce
good sprinkling of Maldon or other sea
  salt, to taste
celery stick or two

Pour all the ingredients, except for the celery sticks, into a pitcher and use a celery stick to stir, then leave it in the pitcher: Bloody Mary needs a stir before each pouring.

Makes approximately 3 half-pint glasses, so be prepared to replenish.

APPLE AND BLACKBERRY KUCHEN

Kuchen may be simply "cake" in German, but what it means in America, taken there by German refugees, is a sweet, but not too sweet, yeast dough, baked in a slab and topped as desired with fruit, nuts or both or neither—to be eaten at breakfast or any time with a cup of coffee. This version has a slightly Anglo-taste: apple and blackberry with a buttery crumble topping. It's unquestionably good as is, but you might consider dolloping some thick, plain yogurt over it as you eat.

If making yeast dough at breakfast time seems unfathomably demanding, relax in the knowledge that you can make this before you go to bed in the evening, leaving it to rise slowly in the refrigerator overnight. That way, all you need to do in the morning is preheat the oven, take the dough out of the refrigerator, let it get to room temperature, then knock it back and press it out over the pan, following on from there.

for the cake base:
2¼ to 2⅓ cups white bread flour
½ teaspoon salt
2 tablespoons sugar
½ package (¼-ounce package) rapid-rise yeast (about 1 teaspoon)
2 eggs
½ teaspoon vanilla extract
grated zest of half a lemon
¼ teaspoon ground cinnamon
½ cup lukewarm milk
scant ¼ cup butter, softened
13 x 9-inch jellyroll pan

for the topping:
1 egg beaten with a tablespoon of cream and a pinch of ground cinnamon
1 small or ½ medium firm, tart apple (approx. 6 ounces in weight)
1⅔ cups blackberries
zest of ½ lemon
⅓ cup self-rising flour
2 tablespoons ground almonds
¼ teaspoon ground cinnamon
scant ¼ cup cold unsalted butter, diced
2 tablespoons granulated sugar
2 tablespoons Demerara, or granulated brown sugar
2 tablespoons sliced almonds

Put 2¼ cups of the flour in a bowl with the salt, sugar and yeast. In another bowl, beat the eggs and add them, with the vanilla extract, lemon zest and cinnamon, to the lukewarm milk. Stir the liquid ingredients into the dry ingredients to make a medium-soft dough, being prepared to add more flour as necessary. I generally use about 2⅓ cups in all, but advise you to start off with the smaller amount: just add more as needed. Work in the soft butter and knead by hand for about 10 minutes or half that time by machine. When the dough is ready it will appear smooth and springy: it suddenly seems to plump up into glossy life.

Cover with a kitchen towel and leave till doubled in size (an hour to an hour and a quarter). Or leave to rise slowly in a cold place overnight. Then punch down and press to line a jellyroll pan measuring 13 × 9 inches. You may think it's never going to stretch to fit, but it will, although you may need to let it rest for 10 minutes or so mid-stretch, especially if the dough has had a cold rise. When it's pressed out on the pan, leave it to rest for 15–20 minutes and then brush with the egg and cream mixture.

Meanwhile, preheat the oven to 400°F. Peel and chop the apple and toss it in a bowl with the blackberries and the zest from the other half lemon. Set aside in the bowl for the few minutes it takes to make the crumble topping. Put the flour, ground almonds and cinnamon in a medium-sized bowl, stir to combine, then add the cold, diced butter. Using the tips of your fingers—index and middle stroking the fleshy pads of your thumbs—rub the butter into the flour. Stop when you have a mixture that resembles clumpy (this is a *very* buttery mixture) oatmeal. Fork in the sugars and flaked almonds.

Tumble the fruit over the egg-washed dough and then sprinkle the crumble on top of that. Put in the oven for 15 minutes, then turn down to 350°F and cook for a further 20 minutes or so, until the dough is swelling and golden at its billowing edges and the crumble is set; don't expect it to be crunchy.

Remove from the oven and, if you can, wait five minutes or so before cutting it into greed-satisfying slabs.

Serves 8–10.

NOTES

NOTES

CHAPTER TWO

COMFORT FOOD

If I'm being honest, for me all food is comfort food, but there are times when you need a bowlful of something hot or a slice of something sweet just to make you feel that the world is a safer place. We all get tired, stressed, sad or lonely, and this is the food that soothes.

MASHED POTATOES

No, I haven't gone mad, thinking you need a recipe for mashed potatoes, it's just that I couldn't even broach the subject of comfort food without starting off here. Plus, there are pointers, suggestions I want to make to ease the labor involved. The first is, buy a potato ricer. It's a cheap, handheld contraption with a punctured base and a lid that you press down. You put the cooked potato in, squeeze, and out come white worms of fluffy mash—as you can see. The beauty is that you don't need to peel the potato. The skin, or most of it—and you can pick up the few straggly bits that get through the net—stays inside the ricer. Otherwise, if it's a necessary bowl of mashed potatoes just for one that you're after, I suggest you bake the potatoes for 1–1½ hours at 425°F and then just scrape out the flesh and fork it fluffy in a bowl with the milk and butter: greater expenditure on fuel but very little in effort. Plus you get to eat the crunchy skins: divine with a good sprinkling of sea salt and a dribble of extra-virgin olive oil.

Mashed potatoes always seem to taste best if the milk or cream you add to them is warm; I just stick a glass measuring cup in the microwave with the milk and butter and heat for a minute or so and then pour in while beating. And even if you're using a potato ricer, you do need to beat. A wooden spoon will do: the point is you need to get air into the potatoes.

I hesitate before giving quantities, so please regard the specifications here as the merest guidelines. This is about how much you need per person, but then, I would not be appalled to eat a bowl of mash myself made from a pound raw weight of potatoes. It may well be, too, that you don't like your mashed potatoes as buttery and creamy as I do; I have learned that there are many people with more austere tastes than mine, though I'm not sure here is the place to indulge them. And—as seems to be the rule with cooking—the more people you have eating, the less per head they seem to need.

9–12 ounces of all-purpose potatoes, per person	**approx. ¼ cup unsalted butter**
approx. ⅓ cup warm milk or cream	**salt and pepper, preferably white**
	freshly grated nutmeg

Boil the halved or chunked (but unpeeled) potatoes in a large pan of lightly salted water. When they are soft enough to mash, drain them thoroughly then push the potato pieces through a potato ricer.

With a wooden spoon, beat in the warm milk or cream and butter and season with salt, pepper and some freshly grated nutmeg to taste. Eat alone and straight from the bowl for the quintessential comfort food.

SALMON FISH CAKES

This is one of the most comforting suppers I know and has the great virtue of being both a cupboard standby and a useful way of using leftover mashed potatoes. A useful way, too, of using up cold boiled potatoes—just push them through the potato ricer and proceed as normal. If the mashed potatoes have been very buttery and soft to start with they will be harder to mold, but not impossible; you may just find you need to give a sturdier coating of matzo meal before frying. Talking of which, I often do this somewhat differently than specified here: I make the patties, then freeze them (on a plastic-wrap–lined baking sheet) until hard, then bag them up; when I want to eat them, I dip them, stonily unthawed, into the egg and matzo meal, fry them on both sides in hot oil until golden and then sit them on a paper towel on a baking sheet in an oven preheated to 250°F for about 40 minutes or until warmed through. And you could leave them here for about 3 hours without doing any damage.

The reason I use matzo meal rather than bread crumbs is that I find store-bought bread crumbs horrible and I am presuming that for an undemanding recipe like this, you are not going to want to plan ahead and busy yourself making them from fresh. Matzo meal is now anyway widely available at supermarkets, and well worth keeping on hand. And I use canned salmon here because I think, strangely enough, that's how they taste best, and it means you can have the wherewithal for these about the place at all times. I do have to warn, though, that the unfried mixture smells absolutely vile. Just hold on to the thought that, once cooked, it tastes wonderful. And with these fat bronzed coral slabs, I suggest frozen peas and ketchup. I don't even like ketchup much, but just as with shepherd's pie, it's an essential here.

for the fish cakes:
1½–2¼ cups cold mashed potatoes
14–15 ounces canned salmon, preferably
    organic
1 tablespoon unsalted butter, melted
    (if the mashed potato hasn't got any
    butter in it)
fat pinch cayenne pepper
grated zest of ½ lemon

salt and pepper
1 egg

for coating and frying:
2 eggs
scant ½ cup matzo meal, preferably
    medium
scant ¼ cup unsalted butter
2 tablespoons vegetable oil

In a large bowl, and preferably with your hands, mix together all the fish cake ingredients.

Cover a baking sheet with plastic wrap, plunge your hands back into the mixture and form fat, palm-sized patties. Place these on the baking sheet and stand in the refrigerator to firm up for about 20 minutes to an hour—or considerably longer if that helps.

Beat the eggs in a shallow soup bowl and sprinkle the matzo meal onto a dinner plate. One by one, dip the fish cakes into the beaten egg and then into the matzo meal, sprinkling and dredging over as you go to help coat them. When you're all done, put the butter and oil in a large frying pan, heat till it begins to fizzle and then fry the fish cakes on each side until the crusts are golden, and speckled brown in parts, and the soothing centers are warmed through.

Makes 7–9 3-inch diameter fish cakes.

DOUBLE POTATO AND HALLOUMI BAKE

I first made this for a piece I was writing for *Vogue* on the mood-enhancing properties of carbohydrates, as promoted by such books as—and how's this for a title?—*Potatoes not Prozac*. The fact that shortly after filing the article I went on a low-carbohydrate diet should not worry us too much here, for I should say that no one has eaten this without being mad for it. It's a simple idea, and as simple to execute. What's more, there's a balance between the components—bland and sweet potatoes, almost-caramelized onion and garlic, more juicy sweetness with the peppers and then the uncompromising plain saltiness of the halloumi (which is mint-flavored sheep's-milk cheese sold mainly in Turkish, Greek or specialty markets)—that seems to add to the eater's equilibrium in turn. You could substitute feta, or do without the cheese altogether if you wanted to serve this as a side dish to roast chicken, say, but in which case be generous with the sea salt once the disk comes out of the oven.

And forgetting about pseudo-scientific and other optimistic theories for a while, this is so upliftingly beautiful to look at: real good-mood colors.

1 large sweet potato
1 large red/firm potato
1 red onion
1 yellow pepper
1 red pepper
½ head of garlic

4 tablespoons olive oil
black pepper
4½ ounces halloumi cheese, sliced as
   thinly as you can
ovenproof 2-quart casserole

Preheat the oven to 400°F.

Cut the sweet potato into rough 1½-inch cubes and the red potato slightly smaller (1-inch cubes) as the sweet potato will cook more quickly. Halve the red onion, then cut each half into 4–6 segments, discarding any tough outer skin. Seed the peppers and cut into 1-inch squares, and separate the cloves of garlic. Put everything into a casserole or whatever you want to use (it should be big, otherwise use two dishes) and, using your hands, give the vegetables a good coating of olive oil. Season with black pepper, but no salt as the cheese will make it salty (and anyway, the salt will make water leach out). Cook for 45 minutes, by which time the vegetables should be cooked through and here and there tinged with brown. You'll need to turn the oven up to maximum or light the broiler for the endgame: so place the thinly sliced cheese on top of the bake, and put it back in the very hot oven or under the broiler until the cheese has melted and turned slightly brown on top, about 5–10 minutes. Serve straight out of the roasting pan.

Serves 2–3.

CHICKEN SOUP AND MATZO BALLS

Yes, this is quite a bother to make (although it's time-consuming rather than laborious, which is a significant distinction), but there is nothing more comforting to eat. This isn't tribal sentiment; for all that it's known as Jewish Penicillin, I wasn't raised on it, but eating it makes me feel I should have been, that indeed we all should have been. (That scientists have recently found chicken broth to contain anti-inflammatory and antibacterial properties is interesting for those on the lookout for nonpatented flu remedies, but true believers—culinary as much as devotional—never needed any such corroboration.)

What we ate at home, rather, was boiled chicken with rice, and I suppose for that reason I like rice in the soup, if it's to have anything—though it truly is at its best as a pure, gold, soothing liquid. But actually it is traditional to sully its purity with starch: go for *lokshen* (vermicelli) or matzo balls, which are best described as cracker-meal dumplings. I always used to think that in order to appreciate these you really needed to have been brought up on them. I wasn't and remained resistant. But I've since found that they do not have to be the digestion-challenging cannonballs that tradition all but decrees. (Not, you understand, that stodge, in this context, is exactly bad.) Just make sure to whisk the egg well before adding the other ingredients, and what you come up with are toothsome dumplings that are soothingly fluffy as well as comfortingly substantial. So I'm happy to give you my friend Olivia Lichtenstein's recipe for them and urge you to get mixing and rolling. The fat used should be *schmalz* (chicken fat), which will be available at any kosher butcher's; failing that—dietary laws considered—it should be goose fat or margarine. But at the risk of offending the laws of Leviticus—and forget risk, it's a dead certainty here— I use butter. But, you know, schmalz is not hard to make: just pluck out the gobbets of chicken fat that cluster just inside the cavity and melt them in a small pan over low heat. That should be more than enough to provide the two tablespoons required here.

As for the chicken in your pot: it really has to be a boiler. A boiling chicken yields up flavor like nothing else, and its flesh needs long cooking, so it doesn't go stringy after hours of boiling. If you can't get hold of a boiling chicken, then you'll have to use a roasting one, but don't cook it for more than an hour and a half. You can then take the meat off the bones, put the carcass back in the stock and carry on cooking it, though you may still need to bump up the flavor; in which case, I'd recommend a slug or two of concentrated chicken bouillon or broth.

For some reason, chicken soup seems to get hotter than any other liquid known to humankind: unless you're careful, you'll sear your throat before you soothe it. But soothe it you truly will: this is amazingly restorative stuff.

**2 small or 1 large boiling or roasting
  chicken(s)**
1 unpeeled onion, halved
1 rib celery
2 carrots, peeled and chunked

a few stalks of parsley
a few peppercorns
2 bay leaves
1 tablespoon salt

Put all the ingredients in a large stockpot, cover abundantly with water, and bring to the boil. Skim to remove all the gray scum that will float to the surface, then let cook at a simmer for about 3 hours. Just keep tasting: when the broth tastes golden and chickeny, it's ready. Remove the chicken and, if you like, leave the soup to get cold so you can remove any fat that collects on the surface. That way you accrue some schmalz, too.

Reheat the stock, and serve it as a plain soup, or add a few carrot sticks—from about 2 carrots, say— and cook in the soup, adding some torn-up pieces of chicken to warm through at the end. I like to add freshly chopped parsley.

Serves 4.

MATZO BALLS

As I said, schmalz you'll have to get from a kosher butcher unless you can render or skim enough from your chicken, but matzo meal is available at supermarkets (I prefer to use the medium rather than the fine ground). It's worth trying these dumplings at least once: there are days when only stodge will do. And, to be fair, made properly, these aren't heavy so much as dense: I am relying on your charity to appreciate the distinction here.

1 egg
**2 tablespoons schmalz, margarine or
  butter, melted**

3 tablespoons water or soup stock
scant 1/2 cup medium matzo meal
pinch of salt and a grind of pepper

Whisk the egg in a large-ish bowl, then whisk in the melted schmalz (or whatever). Carry on whisking as you add the water or soup stock, the matzo meal and salt and pepper, and mix together into a rough paste; if it's too stiff to feel that it might be malleable later, add a little more water. Put in the refrigerator to chill for an hour (or leave overnight if you wish) then dig out small lumps of paste and roll them into walnut-sized balls between the palms of your hands. Cook the dumplings in boiling, salted water and simmer for about 40 minutes (you can just cook them directly in the soup, but I'll do anything to preserve its unstarchy clearness). They are cooked when they rise to the surface. Add to the soup, and ladle out generously into waiting bowls.

Makes about 20.

LEMON RISOTTO

This is comfort food on so many levels. For one, risotto has to be one of the most comforting things to eat ever. What's more, although everyone goes on about the finickiness and crucial fine-tuning involved, I find risotto immensely comforting to make: in times of stress, mindless repetitive activity—in this case, 20 minutes of stirring—can really help. What you don't want to do is make risotto for large numbers of people, which is why I've indicated that this serves two (as supper in its entirety); if you want to call it into service as a starter, then reckon on its feeding four.

There is a more personal reason why this is comforting for me. The recipe comes from Anna del Conte (from her *Secrets of an Italian Kitchen* to be exact), and she, beyond any doubt the best Italian foodwriter around, is the person I turn to for bolstering and solace. Just reading her books provides instant, essential nourishment.

2 shallots	needles from 2 small sprigs of fresh
1 rib of celery	rosemary, finely chopped
1/4 cup unsalted butter	1 egg yolk
1 tablespoon olive oil	4 tablespoons grated Parmesan, plus
1 1/3 cups risotto rice, preferably arborio	more to sprinkle
or Vialone Nano	4 tablespoons heavy cream
approx. 1 quart vegetable stock	Maldon or other sea salt to taste
zest and juice of 1/2 unwaxed lemon	good grating pepper, preferably white

Put the shallots and celery into a mini food processor and blitz until they are a finely chopped mush. Heat half the butter, the oil and the shallot and celery mixture in a wide saucepan, and cook to soften the mixture for about 5 minutes, making sure it doesn't stick. Mix in the rice, stirring to give it a good coating of oil and butter. Meanwhile, heat the stock in another saucepan and keep it at the simmering point.

Pour a ladleful of the stock into the rice and keep stirring until the stock is absorbed. Then add another ladleful and stir again. Continue doing this until the rice is al dente. You may not need all of the stock, equally, you may need to add hot water from the kettle.

Mix the lemon zest and the rosemary into the risotto, and in a small bowl beat the egg yolk, lemon juice, Parmesan, cream and pepper.

When the risotto is ready—when the rice is no longer chalky, but still has some bite—take it off the heat and add the bowl of eggy, lemony mixture, and the remaining butter and salt to taste. Serve with more grated Parmesan if you wish, check the seasoning and dive in.

Serves 2.

STOVETOP RICE PUDDING FOR EMERGENCIES

For those days when you just can't wait the three hours for a proper, old-fashioned rice pudding, this is what you need. In fact, it's just a sweet risotto, with warm milk substituted for the stock. This does mean that the rice takes longer to cook—and what's more, you want it rather less al dente than is usually desirable—but it's the best I can offer. Anyway, you can't, on eating this, resent one moment of your stoveside-stirring captivity.

2 3/4 cups whole milk

1 heaping tablespoon unsalted butter

2–3 tablespoons sugar or vanilla sugar

1/4 cup rice, preferably arborio or
   Vialone Nano

1/2 teaspoon good vanilla extract (if not
   using vanilla sugar)

2–3 tablespoons heavy cream,
   the thicker and fattier the better

Heat the milk in a pan that preferably has a lip, which will make pouring easier (or give it a couple of minutes in a plastic or glass measuring cup in the microwave). When it's about to boil (but don't let it), turn off the heat. Melt the butter and a tablespoonful of the sugar in a heavy-based pan. When hissing away in a glorious pale caramelly pool, add the rice and stir to coat stickily. Gradually add the milk, stirring the rice all the time, and letting each swoosh of milk get absorbed into the consequently swelling rice before adding the next bit. To see when it's ready, start tasting at 20 minutes, but be prepared to go on for 35. You may want to add more milk, too (and if the rice tastes cooked before all the milk's absorbed, don't use all of it).

When the rice feels as it should, thick and sticky and creamy, take it off the heat and beat in another tablespoonful of sugar (taste and see if you want yet more), the vanilla, if using, and as much of the cream as you like. Think of this as the *mantecatura*: the final addition to a risotto, to thicken and add fat-globular volume, normally of butter and grated Parmesan; indeed just add butter if you haven't got any cream in the house.

Serves 1.

CHOCOLATE FUDGE CAKE

I have a bad Amazon habit. You know the "when the going gets tough, the tough go shopping" line? Well, the not-so-tough get their retail therapy online. Or I do: when I can't sleep I start ordering books. And I comfort myself twice over by telling myself how useful they are, how they really help my work. I offer this recipe, adapted from a book that in itself soothes, *Tish Boyle's Diner Desserts*, bought at about 3 A.M. one unravelingly wakeful night, as proof.

This is the sort of cake you'd want to eat the whole of when you've been dumped. But even the sight of it, proud and tall and thickly iced on its stand, comforts.

for the cake:
2²/₃ cups all-purpose flour
³/₄ cup plus 1 tablespoon granulated
   sugar
¹/₃ cup light brown sugar
¹/₄ cup best-quality cocoa powder
2 teaspoons baking powder
1 teaspoon baking soda
¹/₂ teaspoon salt
3 eggs
¹/₂ cup plus 2 tablespoons sour cream
1 tablespoon vanilla extract

³/₄ cup unsalted butter, melted and
   cooled
¹/₂ cup corn oil
1¹/₃ cups chilled water

for the fudge icing:
6 ounces bittersweet chocolate, minimum
   70% cocoa solids
1 cup plus 2 tablespoons unsalted butter,
   softened
1³/₄ cups confectioners' sugar, sifted
1 tablespoon vanilla extract

Preheat the oven to 350°F.

Butter and line the bottom of two 8-inch cake pans.

In a large bowl, mix together the flour, sugars, cocoa, baking powder, baking soda and salt. In another bowl or wide-necked measuring cup whisk together the eggs, sour cream and vanilla until blended. Using a standing or handheld electric mixer, beat together the melted butter and corn oil until just blended (you'll need another large bowl for this if using the hand mixer; the standing mixer comes with its own bowl), then beat in the water. Add the dry ingredients all at once and mix together on a slow speed. Add the egg mixture, and mix again until everything is blended and then pour into the prepared tins. And actually, you could easily do this manually; I just like my toys and find the KitchenAid a comforting presence in itself.

Bake the cakes for 45–50 minutes, or until a cake-tester comes out clean. Cool the cakes in their pans on a wire rack for 15 minutes, and then turn the cakes out onto the rack to cool completely.

To make the icing, melt the chocolate in the microwave—2–3 minutes on medium should do it—or in a bowl sitting over a pan of simmering water, and let cool slightly.

In another bowl beat the butter until it's soft and creamy (again, I use the KitchenAid here) and then add the sifted confectioners' sugar and beat again until everything's light and fluffy. I know sifting is a pain, the one job in the kitchen I really hate, but you have to do it or the icing will be unsoothingly lumpy. Then gently add the vanilla and chocolate and mix together until everything is glossy and smooth.

Sandwich the middle of the cake with about a quarter of the icing, and then ice the top and sides, too, spreading and smoothing with a rubber spatula.

Serves 10. Or 1 with a broken heart.

NOTES

NOTES

CHAPTER THREE

TV DINNERS

Even if you like cooking, at the end of a long day you don't necessarily have much time or energy for it. Of course you can always phone for a pizza, but I find that a bit of pottering in the kitchen helps me unwind. What I'm talking about here is the food you can cook on those days when you just have to hit the kitchen running. . . .

MOZZARELLA IN CARROZZA

This is Italian food before Tuscan rustic chic. The "in carrozza" bit means "in a carriage" and doesn't really explain what this golden-crusted fried mozzarella sandwich is about, just gives an indication that the milky cheese is somehow contained. What you should know if you've never tried it (apart from the fact that it is one of the easiest, most gratifying laptop dinners imaginable) is that it is somewhere between French toast and grilled cheese. For children (and do bear this in mind for a quick, hot filler when they get back from school) it is desirably like a pizza sandwich, and could be made more so with tomato sauce smeared within the bread's tender interior.

It works, as well, served with a tomato or, for adults, chilli sauce alongside, into which you can dip the corners of the oozing sandwich as you eat. And, unorthodox though this is, I love it with a fierce sprinkling of chopped fresh red chilli in with, and to counter, the gorgeously melting blandness of the mozzarella.

I can't pretend this version is absolutely authentic: it wasn't invented using soft white bread. But white sliced is just fine, and, frankly, what I use. For one thing, if you have children it's what you tend to have in the house. Just be sure to use the lightest hand when dunking it in the milk; more than a moment and the bread will have dissolved into unredeemable mushiness. But don't be cautious about this: it's quick and easy to make,

and requires very little in the way of shopping. Speaking of which, it is not worth buying the better, and more expensive, buffalo mozzarella here. The milky dampness of that cheese is not required; it is anyway too liquid and, besides, ordinary cow's-milk mozzarella produces just the right fleshy goo, oozing out of the cut sandwich into stringy, chewy ribbons.

6 slices white bread, crusts removed
1 fist sized ball mozzarella, cut into
  approx. ¼-inch slices, then strips
½ cup whole milk

3 heaping tablespoons all-purpose flour
1 egg
salt and pepper
olive oil (not extra-virgin) for frying

Make sandwiches out of the bread and mozzarella, leaving a little margin around the edges unfilled with cheese, and press the edges together with your fingers to help seal. (One of the advantages of soft white bread is that it is easily smushed together.) Pour the milk into one soup bowl, the flour into another, and beat the egg with salt and pepper in another. Warm the oil in a frying pan over medium heat. Dunk the sandwiches briefly, one by one, in the milk, then dredge in the flour, then dip in the beaten egg. Fry in hot oil on each side till crisp and golden and remove to a paper towel. Cut in half and apply to face.

Serves 2.

CHICKEN WITH CHORIZO AND CANNELLINI

This may sound a kind of fancy thing to be making at the end of a working day, but it is fabulously easy, fabulously quick and everything can be bought at a quick supermarket stop in your lunch hour. Yes, chicken stock is itemized, but I use 2 cups of boiling water to which I've added a tablespoonful or so of chicken bouillon—one of my pantry standbys. If you can't find proper chorizo sausages—the kind that are sold in 8-ounce loops—then buy 4 ounces of slicing chorizo (the salami kind) in one chunk and chop it up into small chunks yourself. And don't worry in the slightest if instead of sprinkling over sweet, smoked paprika at the end, you just use the ordinary kind.

And don't agonize over the chicken cut either. I like to use a supreme (a skinless breast with the peg-bone still attached), but a regular breast would do just fine. Any firm white fish (just replace the chicken stock with fish stock) would be wonderful here, too, instead of the chicken and—as further speed-conscious inducement—would need only about 3 minutes' poaching. Finally, the chorizo and cannellini beans, without any further adornment, are pretty damn good, too. Worth bearing in mind as a way of sprucing up any leftover cold cuts that otherwise stare reproachfully out at you from their refrigerator-bound, plastic-wrap confinement.

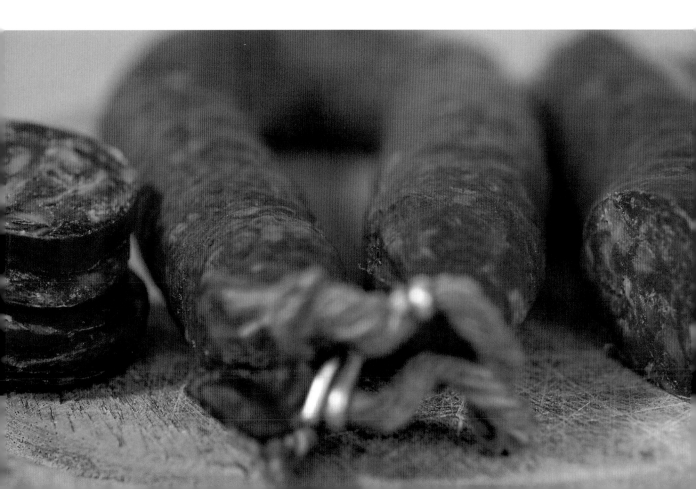

2 cups chicken stock

1 free-range chicken supreme (or skinless breast)

approx. 4½ ounces trimmed kale (generous ½ cup)

1–2 teaspoons olive oil (not extra-virgin)

4 ounces chorizo sausage, sliced then chopped

14 ounces canned cannellini beans, drained

smoked sweet paprika for sprinkling

In a saucepan, bring the stock to a gentle boil, lower in the chicken and cook, still gently, for 10 minutes or until all trace of pink has disappeared. Pierce with the point of a knife to check.

Meanwhile, cook the kale, which you've roughly torn into pieces, in boiling salted water for about 5 minutes (if it's tough) and drain. Then heat the oil in a frying pan, throw in the chopped chorizo, add the drained cannellini and, stirring, warm everything through, moistening with a couple of tablespoons or so of the chicken stock—or more if you want this soupier.

Tip the beans and chorizo into a shallow bowl or lipped plate, roughly arrange the kale on top (drizzling with a little extra-virgin olive oil if you like) and then lift the cooked chicken out of the stock with a spatula and sit this on top of the kale ruff. Sprinkle the pale chicken breast with the paprika and gaze at your Spanish still life of a supper before eating it.

Serves 1.

LINGUINE WITH GARLIC OIL AND PANCETTA

Three ingredients: one great supper. I like this greedily mounded in a bowl and taken up to bed to be eaten, or rather shoveled in, in front of the television. But that's not obligatory.

Good pancetta is not found everywhere (check out butchers and delicatessens), so it makes sense, when you buy it, to get a few 8-ounce blocks. Freeze them separately then just take each one out of the freezer in the morning and return after work to have this fat-striped slab of Italian bacon ready and at your disposal in the evening. Otherwise, you could buy a packet of lardons—those diced bacon cubes—from the supermarket or even use ordinary bacon, snipped into straggly bits. Just bear in mind that cut-up bacon will not need more than about 5 minutes in the hot, aromatic fat to cook.

Of course you could cook the pancetta or bacon in a frying pan, but why I like using the oven is that it needs no supervision. You can put the pancetta in the oven, put the pasta in the boiling, salted water, go up and run yourself a bath (taking your timer with you) and then come down and just drain and toss and dinner's made.

And naturally you can use whatever pasta you like, it's just that linguine (a long pasta that's wider than spaghetti and thicker than tagliatelle) is my favorite—a good reason, it seems to me, to specify it here.

2 tablespoons garlic-infused olive oil　　**8 ounces linguine**
8 ounces pancetta

Preheat the oven to 500°F.

Fill a large saucepan with water and bring to the boil. While it's heating up, put the garlic olive oil in an ovenproof dish; I use an enamel Le Creuset one, measuring 12 x 8 inches. Remove the rind from the pancetta and put it in the dish (to render down: you want as much bacony juices as possible), then dice the rest of the pancetta and add these cubes to the oil, smooshing them about with your fingers to make sure they're equally, if lightly, coated. When the water's boiling, put the dish of garlic-oiled pancetta in the oven,

then salt the boiling water and add the linguine; these should need about 10 minutes to cook. When the pasta's ready, drain it, reserving a scant cupful of the cooking water and take the pancetta dish out of the oven. Tip the drained linguine into the dish and toss well, adding some of the pasta-cooking water, drop by cautious drop, for lubrication as you need it.

And that's it: I like this without Parmesan, but a sprinkling of roughly scissored parsley, should you feel inclined, is always a good idea.

Serves 2.

SALT AND PEPPER SQUID

Just because something's unfamiliar doesn't mean it's hard to cook. OK, I understand that when you think "TV dinner," squid is hardly the first thing to come to mind, but I am asking you to think again. This is unexpectedly easy to shop for as well as easy to cook. Baby squid (better here than tougher, grown-up, windsock-sized ones) can be found, frozen, in 1-pound boxes, to be stashed in your freezer and thawed as needed. And while any recipe that involves a mortar and pestle can seem like too much kitchen fussing when you get back from work, let me tell you that a bit of murderous bashing can be a great stress-relieving exercise. But if you're not convinced (and believe me I understand: until recently I had only to read the words "mortar and pestle" to be filled with dread and intimidation) you can always use one of those little electric coffee-bean or spice grinders for blitzing the salt and pepper. Already-ground pepper and fine salt is not an impossible option; I won't pretend they'll be as good, but as long as you don't use that pepper-container dust—more sneeze-powder than aromatic spice—it'll be just fine.

approx. 2 cups peanut oil (to come about ¹/₂ inch up in a frying pan)

2 tablespoons Maldon or other sea salt

2 tablespoons black peppercorns

¹/₃ cup cornstarch

18 ounces baby squid, cut into rings, tentacles left unchopped

lemon for squeezing

Put the oil in a frying pan over a high heat. Bash the salt and peppercorns in a mortar and pestle till a bit more than bruised but not quite pulverized, and combine this mixture in a freezer bag with the cornstarch, adding the squid and tossing to coat well but not heavily.

When the oil's very hot—not quite smoking but nearly—fry the squid (knocking any excess cornstarch back in the bag first) in batches (about four, probably) and cook each batch for about a minute or so till just crisp on the outside and still sweet and tender within. You probably won't need to turn the squid since the oil should bubble up and cook both sides at once, but do if you feel better. Remove to plates lined with a paper towel. After the squid's sat for about half a minute, remove the greasy towel—though sometimes, I dispense with this stage—squeeze lemon over and eat with your fingers, quickly.

Serves 2.

THAI YELLOW PUMPKIN AND SEAFOOD CURRY

I use the term "TV dinners" loosely. Not everything in this chapter is written with sofa-bound slumping in mind. It's also a good idea to have something up your sleeve that you can cook quickly, and simply, when you've got friends coming over to supper midweek after work. This is that something. Don't let the length of the list of ingredients put you off. You really could go to the supermarket at lunchtime and buy everything you need. What's more, most of it keeps: salmon, raw shrimp, lime leaves and lemongrass in the freezer (and all but the salmon can be used from frozen); curry paste in the refrigerator; the coconut milk, fish sauce, fish-stock concentrate and turmeric in the cupboard. In other words, one shopping expedition, many curries.

Yes, the cilantro you'll need to buy fresh (though at a push you could buy a box of already chopped frozen stuff), as you will the pumpkin or squash and bok choy and—give or take—lime, but whatever, you have the base here for a number of curries. Once you've cooked this and seen both how simple and how divine it is, you'll see how you can adapt it for different produce.

You have to have rice with curry, and the simplest way to cook this is to get an electric rice cooker. The best part of this is that once you've put the rice and water in, the rice cooks itself and—with my model at least—stays warm for 12 hours, so you're not going to have to do any last-minute timing shenanigans. You just stick the rice on when you get in, and it'll be fine whatever time people bowl up for dinner. With the same idea in mind, you should know that you can cook the curry up till the part where the pumpkin is tender and then leave it, reheating it later to cook (for all of about 3 minutes) the shrimp and salmon. Given that most people are late for dinner when they're coming after work, this means that you don't have the dilemma of either leaving something spoiling on the stove or having a frenzied bout of last-minute cooking once they arrive.

I've said 1–2 tablespoons of curry paste. This is because pastes vary enormously in their strengths and people vary enormously in their tastes. Some like it hot: I like it very hot—and use 2 tablespoonfuls. But it might be wiser to add 1 tablespoonful first and then taste later, once all the liquid's in, to see if you want to add more.

One last bossy note: if you can't get raw shrimp, don't use cooked ones; just double the amount of salmon.

14 ounces canned coconut milk (about 1²/₃ cups)

1–2 tablespoons yellow (or red) Thai curry paste

1¹/₂ cups fish stock (I use boiling water and concentrated fish bouillon; cubes would do)

3 tablespoons fish sauce (nam pla)

2 tablespoons sugar

3 lemongrass stalks, each cut into thirds and bruised with the flat of a knife

3 lime leaves, stalked and cut into strips, optional

¹/₂ teaspoon turmeric

2¹/₄ pounds pumpkin or butternut squash, peeled and cut into large, bite-sized chunks

1 pound 2 ounces salmon fillet, preferably organic, skinned and cut into large, bite-sized chunks

1 pound 2 ounces peeled raw shrimp

bok choy or any other green vegetables of your choice

juice of ¹/₂–1 lime, to taste

cilantro, to serve

Skim the thick creamy top off the can of coconut milk and put it, over medium heat, into a large saucepan or casserole with the curry paste. Let it sizzle and, using a fork, whisk or wooden spoon, beat cream and paste together until combined. Still beating gently, add the rest of the coconut milk, fish stock, fish sauce, sugar, lemongrass, lime leaves (if using) and turmeric. Bring to a boil and then add the pumpkin. Cook on a fast simmer until the pumpkin is tender, about 15 minutes, although different sorts of pumpkins can vary enormously in the time they take to cook; some squash take as little as 5 minutes.

As I mentioned, you can cook the curry up till this part in advance, maybe leaving the pumpkin with a tiny bit of bite to it (it will soften and cook as the pan cools). Either way, when you're about 5 minutes away from wanting to eat, get ready to cook the seafood.

So, to the robustly simmering pan, add the salmon and shrimp (if you're using frozen shrimp they'll need to go in before the salmon). When the salmon and shrimp have cooked through, which shouldn't take more than 3–4 minutes, stir in any green vegetable you're using—sliced, chopped or shredded as suits—and tamp down with a wooden spoon. When the bok choy is wilted, or other green vegetable is cooked, squeeze in the juice of half a lime, stir and taste and add the juice of the remaining half if you feel it needs it. Take the pan off the heat or decant the curry into a large bowl, and sprinkle over the cilantro; the point is that the cilantro goes in just before serving. Serve with more chopped cilantro for people to add to their own bowls as they eat, and some plain Thai or basmati rice.

Serves 4–6.

BITTER ORANGE ICE CREAM

I know that suggesting homemade ice cream for an easy after-work supper makes me sound as if I'm going into deranged-superwoman overdrive, but may I put the case for the defense?

All you do to make this is zest and juice some fruit, add confectioners' sugar and cream, whisk and freeze. This requires no stirring or churning and it tastes unlike anything you could buy. So if you've got friends coming over for the curry, you can serve this for dessert to amazed admiration without giving yourself anything approaching a hard time. I use my KitchenAid, but a cheap handheld electric mixer would do fine; and frankly, whisking by hand wouldn't kill you.

I first made this with Seville oranges, but since these are available only in January here, it would be unhelpfully restricting to suggest no substitutes out of season (though you could always freeze the oranges, either whole or just their zest and juice). I won't lie to you and say that my suggested substitutes are quite as magnificent as the original— nothing can provide that biting, aromatic intensity that you get from Seville oranges, which have the taste of orange and the ravaging sourness of lemons—but ordinary eating oranges combined with lime juice provide a glorious tangy and fragrant hit of their own.

3 Seville oranges or 1 eating orange and 2 limes

1 cup plus 2 tablespoons confectioners' sugar

2¹/₂ cups heavy cream

wafers to serve (optional)

If using Seville oranges, grate the zest of 2 of them. Squeeze the juice of all 3 and pour into a bowl with the zest and sugar. If you're going for the sweet orange and lime option, grate the zest of the orange and one of the limes, juice them and add to the sugar as before. Stir to dissolve the sugar and add the heavy cream.

Whip everything until it holds soft peaks, and then turn into a shallow airtight container (of approximately 2 quarts) with a lid. Cover and freeze until firm (from 3 to 5 hours). Remove to ripen for 15–20 minutes (or 30–40 in the refrigerator) before eating. Serve in a bowl, in cones, with wafers—however you like.

Serves 6.

NOTES

CHAPTER FOUR

PARTY GIRL

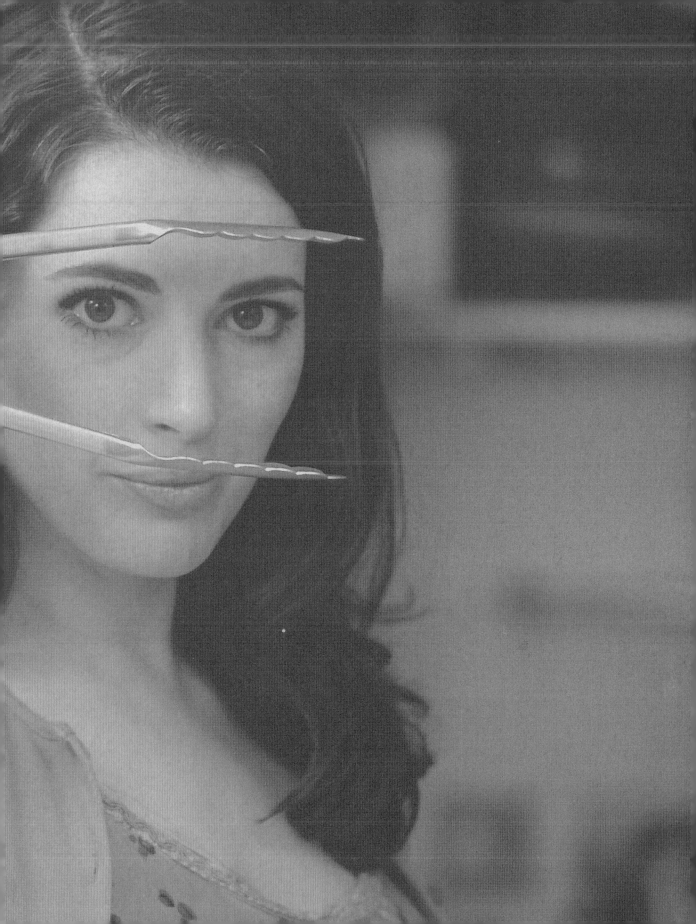

I'd have to go and lie down in a darkened room if I started trying my hand at real party catering, but for children's birthdays or lazily peopled gatherings in a summer garden, there's always food you can do, and that I regularly return to, that actually makes you feel pleased you invited anyone in the first place.

PIGS IN BLANKETS

As far as I know, Pigs in Blankets is a wartime recipe; I first came across it in an old *Woman's Own* cookbook of my grandmother's, but have noticed differing versions of it since. The original I saw was for a chunky parcel—sausages wrapped in a thick potato pastry and then baked, wonderfully true somehow to the evocative title. This is a simplified version made with a fork-mixed cheese scone dough, and a diminutive one, perfectly suited to a children's birthday party or simply to entertain them in the kitchen.

In fact, I use the cooked pork cocktail sausages from a specialty gourmet shop, partly because cooking, cooling, then wrapping sausages seems a bother and partly because this way I'm less tempted to eat them myself. Somehow, though, I still manage.

Anyway, children love them, and they are reassuringly easy to make. In fact, there's nothing about their preparation that even a modestly interested child couldn't cope with.

2 cups plus 5 tablespoons self-rising
  flour
1 heaping teaspoon salt
2 tablespoons grated Red Leicester or
  Cheddar cheese
1 cup whole milk
1 egg

3 tablespoons vegetable oil
50 pork cocktail sausages (mini
  hot dogs)

to glaze:
1 egg, mixed with a splash of milk and
  half a teaspoon of salt

Preheat the oven to 425°F.

Measure the flour into a bowl, add the salt and grated cheese and mix lightly with a fork. Pour the milk into a measuring cup to come up to the 1-cup mark and then crack in the egg and add the oil. Beat to combine, then pour into the dry ingredients, forking to mix as you go. You may, at the end, feel the dough's either too dry or too damp: add either more milk or more flour and fork together again till you've got a soft dough that's not too sticky to be rolled out.

Break the dough into two pieces and roll the first one out onto a lightly floured surface. Scone dough is a dream to work with; in fact, I find it deeply pleasurable. Just roll as clumsily and heavy handedly as you like: no harm will come to it. You want a thin, but not exaggeratedly so, rectangle. A square wouldn't be the end of the world either, so don't start getting out the geometry set: this is the roughest of instructions.

Cut the dough into approximately 1¾-inch strips, and then cut each strip at approximately 2½-inch intervals so that you end up with a collection of small, raggedy oblongs (I just cut each strip as I go, but it's probably more efficient to do the whole batch of dough at one time).

Take a cocktail sausage and put it at one end of an oblong at a slight diagonal

and then roll up, pressing on the infinitely compliant dough to squeeze it shut, and then place on a nonstick baking sheet, or one lined with parchment. Carry on until you've finished all your strips and then get to work with the remaining dough. Three baking sheets should do it.

Now, dip a pastry brush into the beaten egg mixture and paint on a golden glaze. Put in the oven and cook for 12–15 minutes, by which time they should be puffy and burnished. Remove from the oven and let cool a little before giving them to the children.

Makes 50.

LILAC- OR CHOCOLATE-TOPPED CUPCAKES

What's a children's party without cupcakes? In truth, it's better to make mini ones for smaller children; they just like the icing anyway, so there's no point in majoring in the cake. Since we're going through a purple stage at the moment—pink, for us, is *so* last year—I go full out for their garish pleasure by tinting the icing a heart-stopping lilac with a minuscule blob of Grape Violet food-coloring paste. But since adults love cupcakes just as much, I suggest them also as a dessert for a grown-up party—in which case, though, make a chocolate ganache to be smoothed over full-sized cupcakes. In both cases, I decorate with gold buttons, but if you can't find these, shiny M&M's or gold dragees plonked glossily on top would seduce just as well.

For something a little more festive, in the case of the grown-up ones at least (and as an alternative to a traditional birthday cake), forget the central decoration on top and spike each cupcake with a candle and leave to smolder atmospherically for a while on serving. And to make chocolate cupcakes, which in either instance could be thought preferable, take out a tablespoonful of flour after measuring and replace with the same amount of cocoa.

for cupcakes:	*for icing:*
³/₄ cup self-rising flour	approx. 1¹/₄ cups confectioners' sugar,
¹/₂ cup very soft unsalted butter	sifted, or instant royal icing
7 tablespoons sugar	food coloring paste
2 eggs	gold chocolate buttons (or M&M's)
1–2 teaspoons vanilla extract	12-cup cupcake pan or 3 12-cup mini-
few tablespoons whole milk	cupcake pans with appropriately sized
	paper baking cups

Preheat the oven to 400°F.

Put all the ingredients for the cupcakes except the milk into a food processor and blitz furiously. Then pour in the milk, and process again until you have a smooth batter. Divide the mixture between either the big muffin pans or the three small pans.

Cook the big cupcakes for about 15–20 minutes, and the small ones for about 10 minutes, although you might need to keep a closer eye on the little ones. Cool the cupcakes on a wire rack.

To ice the mini-cupcakes, mix the confectioners' sugar with a tablespoon or two of water from a recently boiled kettle or cold water (according to package instructions) for instant royal icing until you have a smooth, spreadable paste. In both cases add water slowly: you don't want this runny, and nothing is more irritating than having to start sifting more sugar. The merest, tiniest blob of food-coloring paste—in this case, as I said, Grape Violet—will be enough to bring a dizzy and rich-toned intensity to the proceedings;

you can always add more coloring if you want, but again the important thing is to guard against having to do any more sifting. And if you have been too heavy-handed and landed yourself with a batch of unusably dark icing, then just make up some more plain white icing and add to tone down.

Slice any peaking humps off the tops of the cakes with a sharp knife and then pour, from a dunked-in spoon, the icing over each cake until the tops are thickly and smoothly covered. Let stand for a couple of minutes until the icing has set a tiny bit and then dot a gold button or other decoration of your choice on top.

CHOCOLATE GANACHE

This is a very useful icing to have up your sleeve for any sort of cake. The quantities here make enough to ice, thickly and glossily, 12 normal-sized cupcakes, but since all a chocolate ganache is is an equal quantity of heavy cream and chocolate heated together, it's easy to increase the volume of icing at your disposal.

I most often use, in cooking (and fall upon for eating), the most fabulous chocolate buttons made by a company called Montgomery Moore: the chocolate itself is incredibly good, and because it's already in buttons you don't have to chop it to make it easy to melt. But, any good-quality bittersweet or semisweet chocolate works well.

7 ounces bittersweet chocolate, with a minimum of 70% cocoa solids, chopped, or use chocolate buttons (see above)

¾ cup plus 2 tablespoons heavy cream

Put both ingredients in a saucepan and, over low heat, cook till the chocolate's melted. Whisk together with handheld mixer or electric whisk (for ease and preference), watching the mixture become thick and glossy. Spoon and smooth over your waiting cupcakes. After a couple of minutes' standing, decorate in whatever way you want.

BAGNA CAUDA

All good parties involve a lot of standing around gossiping and picking, and this is the food you want tableside to be picked from. I am loath to say the word "dip," but this is in effect what *bagna cauda* is, a ravishing Piedmontese velvety gunge of olive oil, garlic, anchovies and melted butter into which are speared raw florets of tight-budded ivory cauliflower, tightly furled chicory leaves, slices of zucchini, fennel, Belgian endive and red or (for aesthetic preference) yellow peppers and any other crudités that you want to provide.

Ideally, you want to keep the sauce warm, and for this you need either the traditional terracotta bowl that sits over a spirit burner or—oh joy of joys—a fondue dish that can be placed over its candle-fitted stand to achieve the same purpose.

½ cup plus 2 tablespoons extra-virgin olive oil

4–5 cloves of garlic, peeled and Microplaned or minced

12 anchovies preserved in olive oil, drained and chopped

⅓ to ½ cup unsalted butter, cut into chunks

for dipping:
a variety of raw vegetables, including fennel, cauliflower, Belgian endive, sweet peppers and zucchini

Put the oil in a pan with the garlic and anchovies and cook over a low heat, stirring, until you have a melted, muddy mess. Everything should begin to meld together. Whisk in 6 tablespoons of butter, and as soon as it has melted, remove from the heat and give a few more beats of your whisk so that everything is creamy and amalgamated. Taste, and if you feel you want this dipping sauce—which is meant to be pungent but not acrid—a little more mellow, whisk in the remaining 2 tablespoons of butter. Pour into a dish that, ideally, fits over a flame so that it does not get cold at the table.

Dip in the crudités and eat.

THE UNION SQUARE CAFÉ'S BAR NUTS

More picking food, and ludicrously easy to make. You might think that nuts, untampered with, are perfect picking food as they are, and up to a point you'd be right. But try these, modestly adapted from the recipe for the spiced nuts served at the Union Square Café in New York, and you'll truly know what perfection is.

2¼ cups (18 ounces) assorted unsalted nuts, including peeled peanuts, cashews, Brazil nuts, hazelnuts, walnuts, pecans and whole unpeeled almonds

2 tablespoons coarsely chopped fresh rosemary

½ teaspoon cayenne pepper

2 teaspoons dark brown sugar

2 teaspoons Maldon or other sea salt

1 tablespoon unsalted butter, melted

Preheat the oven to 350°F.

Toss the nuts in a large bowl to combine and spread them out on a baking sheet. Toast in the oven till they become light golden brown, about 10 minutes.

In a large bowl, combine the rosemary, cayenne, sugar, salt and melted butter.

Thoroughly toss the toasted nuts in the spiced butter and serve warm. And once you eat these, you will never want to stop.

HALLOUMI WITH CHILLI

I love grilled or fried halloumi, that squeaky, salty, polystyrene-textured sheep's-milk cheese. Not a very seductive way of describing it maybe, but that, indeed, is what it's like. You should have no difficulty finding it in cheese shops, Turkish or Greek markets or specialty shops. This is easy to make. You don't need to do it at the very last minute, but don't fry the halloumi so far in advance that it's totally cooled by the time it comes to the table. And if you prefer, by all means broil it. And again, this is the sort of food that you can sit on the table for people idly to eat as they stand around, drink in hand. It looks beautiful, too, which is always an aid to proceedings. If you must, use another cheese such as Munster, Fontina, Gruyere or raclette.

2 tablespoons chopped, seeded fresh red chilli (about 2 medium chillies)

2 tablespoons extra-virgin olive oil

18 ounces halloumi, sliced medium-thin (i.e., just under ¼ inch)

juice of ¼ lemon

Mix the chopped chilli and olive oil in a small bowl or cup and leave the flavors to deepen while you cook the cheese. I use a nonstick frying pan for this, without any oil, and just give the cheese slices about 2 minutes a side until they're golden brown in parts. When all the slices of halloumi are cooked, transfer them to a couple of small plates. Give the chilli oil a stir, spoon it over the cheese, then give a spritz of lemon. That's all there is to it.

Makes about 30.

SPATCHCOCKED BIRDS

For that point in the evening when people need to hunker down to some serious eating, you do need to provide something a little more substantial than plates for picking from. This is what I roll out during a summer evening's barbecuing. You can stick with just chicken if you want, but I've suggested Cornish game hens or poussins and quail as well, just because I like anything that produces that welcoming sense of the groaning board—and plus, it gives me the opportunity to suggest more than one marinade.

The marinades themselves are to be regarded as the loosest blueprints. Use the flavorings you like, remembering that you need oil of some sort to prevent the meat from drying out and an acid—vinegar, citrus fruit—to tenderize it. The spatchcocked birds don't need to be cooked on the grill; an oven preheated to 425°F or 500°F will do just fine. And because the birds are spatchcocked—that's to say, cut on one side and opened out like a book—they need much less cooking than surgically uninterfered-with poultry, which can be useful if you've got time in advance for the spatchcocking and marinading and not much time on the night for actual cooking.

Any good butcher will spatchcock, or butterfly, the birds for you, or you could ask the meat department at the supermarket to do it, but it's easy enough for you to manage yourself at home. Just get a pair of poultry shears or tough scissors (I use a pair sold by someone on one of those door-to-door trails made for cutting through metal and tough stuff) and lay the bird, breast-side down, on a surface and cut all along one side of the backbone. Then cut along the other side and—hey presto—the backbone can be removed. You then turn the bird the other way up and press down as you open it out. You have in front of you a spatchcocked bird, ready for its marinade.

1 spatchcocked or butterflied chicken,
   marinated in:
juice of 1 lemon
2 tablespoons black peppercorns, lightly
   crushed in mortar and pestle
generous 1/3 cup olive oil (not extra-
   virgin)
2 cloves of garlic, peeled and bruised

to sprinkle over:
Maldon or other sea salt
handful of fresh parsley, chopped

2 spatchcocked or butterflied poussins
   or Cornish game hens, marinated in:
juice of 2 limes
2 tablespoons coriander seeds
generous 1/3 cup peanut or vegetable oil
good grinding of black pepper

to sprinkle over:
Maldon or other sea salt
bunch of fresh cilantro, chopped

4 spatchcocked or butterflied quails,
   marinated in:
1 bunch of scallions, sliced finely
generous 1/3 cup vegetable oil
dash of toasted sesame oil
3/4-inch chunk fresh ginger, unpeeled and
   chopped roughly
1 tablespoon rice vinegar
1 tablespoon soy sauce

to sprinkle over:
Maldon or other sea salt
bunch of fresh cilantro, chopped

Sit the birds in their marinade in a dish into which they fit snugly, cover with plastic wrap and leave in the refrigerator, preferably overnight or for 24 hours, though even a couple of hours would have an effect.

When the grill is good and hot, lift the birds out of their marinade and cook until the flesh has lost all raw pinkness but is still tender within and the skin is crisp and burnished and blistered. It's hard to be precise about times, since grills differ even more than ovens do, but on my grill—a gas-fired Outdoor Chef, which I love to distraction and, since it has a lid, I use even in the winter rain—the chicken takes about 35 minutes, the Cornish hens 15 and the quail about 7.

Along with sea salt, sprinkle freshly chopped parsley over the chicken and cilantro over the hens and quail, or use whatever other herb seems right for the marinades you've concocted.

NOTES

NOTES

CHAPTER FIVE

RAINY DAYS

So much emphasis these days is put on quickly prepared food and skin-of-your-teeth cooking—which is fine, good even, for every day, but if the point of cooking is the end product, its meaning has to lie in the process. And sometimes, on housebound rainy weekends or when you need to savor a little domestic warmth, you want to inhabit your kitchen, not merely rush through it.

PASTA WITH MEATBALLS

This is definitely time-consuming, but here I make no apology for that. And there is nothing like serving up a bowl of pasta with meatballs to make you feel like an Italian mama out of a Hollywood film. I don't mean one of those redoubtable types in amorphous black: think Sophia Loren in the kitchen. It works for me.

The trick to these meatballs is to keep them small. Don't actually use a teaspoon, but use about a teaspoon's amount of ground meat to roll each ball. If there are children around, so much the better; they tend to like making these. But otherwise, they're easy enough, and the slow repetitiveness of the action can be rather calming.

for the meatballs:

9 ounces ground pork

9 ounces ground beef

1 egg

2 tablespoons freshly grated Parmesan

1 garlic clove, minced

1 teaspoon dried oregano

3 tablespoons fine bread crumbs

good grind of black pepper

1 teaspoon salt

Just put everything in a large bowl and then, using your hands, mix to combine before shaping into small balls. Place the meatballs on baking sheets or plates that you have lined with plastic wrap, and put each in the refrigerator as you finish them.

for the tomato sauce:

1 onion

2 cloves garlic

1 teaspoon dried oregano

1 tablespoon unsalted butter

1 tablespoon olive oil (not extra-virgin)

24 ounces canned tomatoes in purée

¾ cup water

pinch of sugar

salt and pepper

⅓ cup plus 1 tablespoon whole milk

Put the onion, garlic and oregano into the processor and blitz to a pulp. Heat the butter and oil in a deep, wide pan, then scrape the onion-garlic mix into it and cook over low to medium heat for about 10 minutes. Don't let the mixture stick, just let it become soft. Add the tomatoes and then add about ¾ cup cold water to the pan with the pinch of sugar and some salt and pepper, and cook for about 10 minutes. The tomato sauce may appear thin at this stage, but don't worry, as it will thicken a little later. Stir in the milk, and then drop the meatballs in one by one. Don't stir the pan until the meatballs have turned from pink to brown, as you don't want to break them up. Cook everything for about 20 minutes, with the lid only partially covering it. At the end of cooking time, check the seasoning, as you may want more salt and a grind or two more of pepper.

Makes enough to sauce generously the pasta that follows, serving 6.

PASTA

To go with these divine meatballs, I like tagliatelle. De Cecco, Spinosi or Cipriani brands are all very good, but making fresh pasta is an experience worth trying. No one's saying you *have* to make it, but once you try, you'll soon see that it's not difficult. I had a pasta machine for years before I was brave enough to use it; for some reason I thought it would be a performance. But I tried and it isn't, and I rather like the mood of peaceful concentration the activity ushers forth. And it's a great way of playing in the kitchen with children: they love turning the handle, which is actually a help, not often the case when the children are cooking with you.

Quantities are easy so long as you remember you need 1 egg per ½ cup of pasta or 00 flour (now available at most supermarkets), and that, on average, one "egg" of pasta, as it were, feeds two generously.

2 cups pasta or Italian 00 flour   **4 eggs**
fat pinch of salt

Either put the flour (with the salt) in a bowl and crack the eggs into it, or make a mound of flour on a worktop and add the eggs to that. I don't bother to beat them before adding them to the flour, but if you prefer to, do. Just find the way that you prefer. All you do is mix the flour and eggs together, and then knead the mixture until it all comes together in a satiny mass. Kneading involves no more than pushing the mixture away from you with the heels of your hands and then bringing it back toward you. If you've got an electric mixer with a dough hook, then use that, though for some reason I don't find it makes the pasta cohere any sooner. And you don't get the relaxing satisfaction of making it by hand.

When the pasta is silky and smooth, form it into a ball, cover with a cloth and leave for 30 minutes to an hour. Then get out your pasta machine, read the instructions and away you go. Two tips first: cut each slice you want to feed through the pasta machine as you go, and put through the no. 1 press quite a few times, folding the strip in half and pushing it through again after each time. When the pasta dough's been fed a few times through the no. 1 slot, pass it through the remaining numbers on the gauge before pushing it through the tagliatelle-cutters. And I find that the pasta strips cut into tagliatelle better if you leave them hanging over the table or wherever to dry a little first (10 minutes is enough).

When you cook the pasta, make sure you've got plenty of boiling, salted water and start tasting as soon as the water comes back to the boil after you've put the pasta in. Use about a third of the meatballs in their sauce to toss with the cooked, drained pasta and then pour the rest of them over the scantly sauced ribbons in the bowl. This is ambrosia: food to get you through the winter happily.

Serves 4–6.

SOFT AND SHARP INVOLTINI

I often make a southern Italian dish of involtini: eggplant, sliced thinly, lightly fried and cooled, and then wrapped around a mixture of basil, pine nuts, bread crumbs, garlic, provolone and Parmesan, bound with egg, then baked in tomato sauce dotted with mozzarella. It's fiddly, but not difficult, and perfect for those times when you have the desire for a bit of slow pottering about in the kitchen. It also happens, as does this version, to be an incredibly useful standby for vile meat eaters like me who want to have something for vegetarians at a dinner party or whatever.

I've still called this involtini, although in truth there is nothing Italian about its component parts. The flavors are more Greek in nature: sharp feta, which perfectly offsets the soft sweetness of the eggplant; and oregano, which is, dried and aromatic, *the* herb of the Greek islands. It also occurred to me that using a dried herb made this a useful, year-round regular. In fact, it was my vegetarian option at my Christmas lunch last year.

I tend to do this in stages: the tomato sauce and eggplant one day; the stuffing, wrapping and baking the next. And I love it at room temperature the next day, too.

for the sauce:
1 onion
1 clove garlic
half a teaspoon dried oregano
2 tablespoons olive oil
**40 ounces (approx. 5 cups) canned
    chopped tomatoes**
2 teaspoons sugar
salt and pepper to taste
2 tablespoons extra-virgin olive oil
4 eggplant (4 to 5 pounds total)
**olive oil for painting the eggplant
    (have plenty on hand)**
**ovenproof baking dish, approx. 2-quart
    capacity**

for the stuffing:
scant ½ cup bulgur wheat
1 teaspoon dried oregano
1½ cups boiling water
**scant ¼ cup shelled pistachios, roughly
    chopped**
7 ounces feta cheese, crumbled
1 clove garlic, minced
1 fat or 2 thin scallions, finely sliced
2 tablespoons capers (drained of brine)
1 egg
a pinch of cinnamon

for the top:
3 ounces feta cheese, crumbled
drizzle of olive oil
fat pinch of dried oregano

Peel and roughly chop the onion and press on the garlic with the flat of a knife to loosen the skin. Remove it and then sling onion, garlic and dried oregano into a food processor and blitz to a pulp. Cook in a deep, generous-sized pan (with a lid) in the 2 tablespoons of olive oil, over a medium to low heat, until softened—about 7 minutes. Add the tomatoes and the sugar, stir well, cover and turn down the heat, and let cook for about 20 minutes, checking often to see that the sauce is not bubbling too vociferously (and therefore sticking or drying out, or indeed both). Taste for seasoning, add salt and pepper or maybe a pinch more sugar if you feel it needs it, then stir again, add the extra-virgin olive oil, and take off the heat but keep the cover on. Leave till you need it.

Cut the eggplant in thinnish slices lengthwise and chuck away the two skin-covered edges: you need to be able to roll the eggplant lengths up later and so you need the full extent. It may sound wasteful, but I'm happy if I get 4–5 good slices per eggplant. Put some oil into a bowl and using a pastry brush, paint each slice generously with the oil. Then cook them on a hot griddle until bronzed, striped without and tender within. Or you can just fry the eggplant slices in a pan filled to about half an inch depth of olive oil. In either case, remove the cooked slices to sheets of paper towel to absorb excess oil. Cook all the eggplant slices this way and then, when cool, you can either begin the stuffing and rolling, or set them aside until you want to. If I'm doing this in advance, I line a dish with baking parchment, arrange a layer of eggplant slices on top, then cover with parchment, then another layer of eggplant and so on, until I've packed them all away. Cover with a layer of parchment and leave till needed.

I tend to stuff the eggplant shortly before cooking them. Measure the bulgur wheat into a bowl, add the dried oregano, pour over the water and cover with a plate. Leave to steep for 30 minutes. Meanwhile, preheat the oven to 375°F, and oil your oven-proof dish lightly.

When the bulgur wheat has had its time, pour it into a large sieve and press down to remove excess water. Leave for a few minutes till it's cooled a little and then decant to a large bowl. Add about two-thirds of the chopped pistachios (you just need to leave some for sprinkling when serving), the crumbled feta, minced garlic, scallions and capers. Stir to mix, but don't be too heavy-handed about it: a few goes with a fork should be enough to combine everything. Beat the egg with the cinnamon and fork this in, too. I find it easier after that's done just to weigh in with my hands, squeezing everything together so you've got a cohesive, nubbly stuffing in front of you.

Get out the eggplant and, one by one, place them in front of you, stalk end at the top, bulbous bottom nearest you. Add a dollop of stuffing at the bottom, roll up lengthwise away from you and put each fat little bundle in the oiled dish as you go. When they're all sitting there snuggly, pour over the tomato sauce, scatter over the crumbled feta for the topping, drizzle with oil, sprinkle over a little dried oregano and cook for 30 minutes. Remove from the oven and let stand at least 15 minutes before serving: this shouldn't be piping hot. Scatter with the remaining pistachios before bringing it to the table.

Serves 4 as a main course; 12 rolls.

PASTA E FAGIOLI

This is that life-saving, thick, pasta-and-bean meal of a soup as sung about by Dean Martin in "That's Amore." It's just the thing you want to eat when the rain's battering against the windowpanes and just what you need to cook to make you feel that you're safe and warm, happy and occupied within.

I have to say, it's the first time I've included a knee-high hosiery sock among any list of ingredients. By all means bundle the rosemary and onion into cheesecloth if it makes you feel more satisfactorily homespun, but I am just not one of those efficiently traditional domestic types that keeps cheesecloths and muslins on hand.

3 cups (about 18 ounces) dried
   cranberry beans
5 cloves of garlic, whole, plus 1,
   Microplaned or grated
1 knee-high hosiery sock
2 leafy sprigs of rosemary
1 onion, peeled and quartered
salt to taste

1 tablespoon tomato paste
3 tablespoons olive oil
sprig of rosemary, about 2 inches,
   needles finely chopped
7 ounces ditalini, tubetti or other small
   pasta tubes
extra-virgin olive oil, to serve

Put the cranberry beans in a large bowl, cover with cold water and let the beans soak overnight or for at least 6 hours.

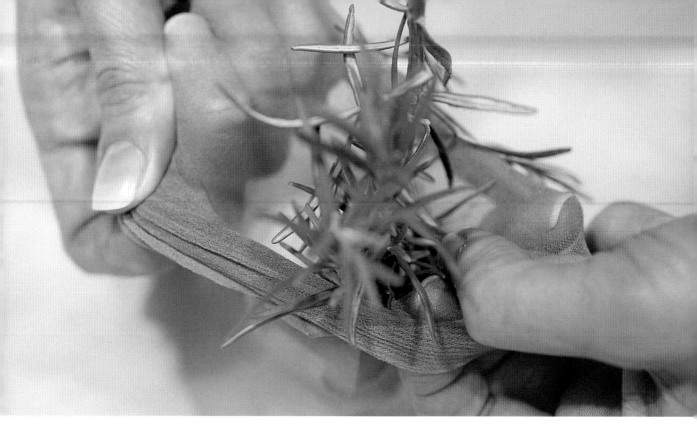

Drain the beans and tip them into a large saucepan. Using the flat side of a large knife, press down on the whole garlic cloves so that their papery skins tear and begin to come away. Peel them and chuck the bruised cloves on top of the beans. Now take your knee-high and in it pop the sprigs of rosemary and cut-up onion. This will stop the needles (which turn bitter on boiling) from infiltrating the soup (very irritating between the teeth, too) but allow their resiny fragrance to seep through. I also find it better not to have slimy onion skins all over the place later. Cover everything generously with cold water, clamp on a lid and bring to the boil. Once it's started boiling, turn the heat down and simmer for an hour. Check the beans to see how cooked they are and, only when they're tender, add salt to taste.

Chuck out the corpsed knee-high and its contents. Remove a mugful of beans—or more if you want a very thick soup—and tip into a blender (my preference) or processor, along with a tablespoonful of tomato concentrate and 1¼ cups of the bean-cooking liquid and liquidize.

Now, add the 3 tablespoons of oil to a small saucepan and grate (I always use my fine Microplane for this) or squeeze in the sixth clove of garlic. Cook over a low to medium heat until soft but not colored and then stir in the finely chopped rosemary. Cook for another scant minute, add the liquidized soup and cook for a minute or so, then tip into the large pan of beans. Bring back to the boil and add the ditalini, cooking them according to package instructions. Drizzle with extra-virgin olive oil and serve.

Serves 8.

CHOCOLATE CLOUD CAKE

On days when I want the warmth of the hearth rather than the hurly-burly of the city streets I stay in and read cookbooks, and this recipe comes from just the sort of book that gives most succor, *Classic Home Desserts* by Richard Sax. The cake itself (which was the dessert I made for last New Year's Eve dinner) is as richly and rewardingly sustaining: a melting, dark, flourless, chocolate base, the sort that sinks damply on cooling; the fallen center then cloudily filled with softly whipped cream and sprinkled with cocoa powder. As Richard Sax says, "Intensity, then relief, in each bite."

9 ounces bittersweet chocolate,
 minimum 70% cocoa solids
½ cup unsalted butter, softened
6 eggs: 2 whole, 4 separated
½ cup plus 1 tablespoon sugar
2 tablespoons Cointreau (optional)
grated zest of 1 orange (optional)
9-inch springform cake pan

for the cream topping:
2 cups heavy cream
1 teaspoon vanilla extract
1 tablespoon Cointreau (optional)
½ teaspoon unsweetened cocoa
 powder for sprinkling

Preheat the oven to 350°F.

Line the bottom of the cake pan with baking parchment.

Melt the chocolate either in a double boiler or a microwave, and then let the butter melt in the warm chocolate.

Beat the 2 whole eggs and 4 egg yolks with ⅓ cup of the sugar, then gently add the chocolate mixture, the Cointreau and the orange zest.

In another bowl, whisk the 4 egg whites until foamy, then gradually add the remaining sugar and whisk until the whites hold their shape but are not too stiff. Lighten the chocolate mixture with a dollop of egg whites, and then fold in the rest of the whites. Pour into the prepared pan and bake for 35–40 minutes or until the cake is risen and cracked and the center is no longer wobbly. Cool the cake in its pan on a wire rack; the middle will sink as it cools.

When you are ready to eat, place the still pan-bound cake on a cake stand or plate for serving and carefully remove the cake from its pan. Don't worry about cracks or rough edges: it's the crater look we're going for here. Whip the cream until it's soft and then add the vanilla and Cointreau and continue whisking until the cream is firm but not stiff. Fill the crater of the cake with the whipped cream, easing it out gently toward the edges of the cake, and dust the top lightly with cocoa powder pushed through a tea-strainer.

Serves 8–12.

You can make this into an Easter Nest Cake by folding 7 ounces of melted chocolate into the cream topping and dotting with sugar-coated eggs instead of the cocoa. Leave the Cointreau out of both the cake and cream.

RASPBERRY AND LEMONGRASS TRIFLE

Trifle is the perfect thing to cook when you've got protracted time to busy yourself quietly in the kitchen. No one stage takes long, but the whole needs to be lingered over. And if it sounds odd to suggest steeping the ladyfingers in a syrup flavored with lemongrass, I should say that I first had the idea when making a syrup with lemon balm for some jelly. If you've got a garden, this is easy to come by, but if you haven't, there is no way you can buy it. I tried, then, substituting lemongrass, weight for weight, and it worked beautifully. By the same token, if you have got verbena in the garden then do use that here. But since there isn't a supermarket around that doesn't major in lemongrass—and indeed it's far more familiar to us than the indigenous lemon balm—this recipe, which first found shape in an *Observer* article on cooking traditional British foods with new "fusion" ingredients, is actually a good reminder that you can plunder the past without scorning the present.

2¹/₂ cups water

1³/₄ cups sugar

2 ounces lemongrass, 3–4 sticks, cut in
   half lengthwise

1¹/₃ cups raspberries

16 store-bought ladyfingers

3–4 tablespoons vodka

2¹/₂ cups light cream

8 egg yolks

2 cups heavy cream

medium glass bowl

Make a syrup with the water and 1½ cups of the sugar by bringing them to the boil in a saucepan and boiling for 5 minutes. Take the pan off the heat, add the lemongrass and let it infuse for about half an hour.

Strain the syrup into a measuring cup, keeping the saucepan with the lemongrass to one side. Take out about ½ to ¾ cup of the syrup and put it into a pan with the raspberries. Bring it to a rolling boil and let it thicken slightly, mashing the fruit to make a jam-like consistency. Let it cool a little and then dunk the ladyfingers in the raspberry mixture and arrange them in the bottom of your bowl. Add the vodka and about ½ cup of the lemongrass syrup, depending on how much your ladyfingers absorb, and reserve the rest.

Meanwhile, to make the custard, heat the light cream in the syrup pan with the lemongrass until it is nearly boiling, take it off the heat and let it infuse for about 15 minutes. Whisk the yolks and the rest of the sugar together and pour the cream into the same bowl. Then whisk again and put the custard back on the heat in the cleaned-out pan. Stir until the custard thickens and then pour it over the trifle sponges. Let it cool.

Whip the heavy cream until thick but not stiff, and cover the custard layer. Use about 1 cup of the remaining sugar syrup to make a caramel by heating it in a saucepan until it turns a golden brown. Drizzle the caramelized sugar syrup over the layer of cream to decorate.

Serves 8–10.

RAINY-DAY COOKIES

If you've got children, you'll know all about the problems of keeping them occupied when the weather's bad and outdoors is uninviting—if only to you. Actually, I go further than that. I am singularly unathletic and rather dread extended bouts on the swings in the park even on sunny days. Cooking is thus, for me, the easiest childcare option. And even two-year-olds can be usefully entertained with a bit of dough and some cookie cutters. Yes, the kitchen will be a mess, but the afternoon will be gone, and then there's just bath- and bedtime to be got through—then peace: a small price, then.

I wouldn't go so far as to say I collect cookie cutters, but I ask anyone who's going abroad to buy any amusing form they find and seem to have acquired a stash of curious shapes. The ones that were used for the pictures here were from this disorganized jumble and seemed best suited to making cookies to banish rainy-day blues.

3/4 cup soft unsalted butter

3/4 cup light brown sugar

2 eggs

1/4 teaspoon almond extract

2 1/4 cups all-purpose flour (plus more if needed)

scant 1/4 cup ground almonds

1 teaspoon baking powder

1 teaspoon salt

cookie cutters

2 nonstick baking sheets

for the icing:

approx. 2 cups confectioners' sugar

water to mix

paste food coloring

Preheat the oven to 350°F.

Cream the butter and sugar together well until almost mousse-like, then beat in the eggs and almond extract.

In another bowl, combine the flour, ground almonds, baking powder and salt. Gradually add these dry ingredients to the butter and egg mixture and combine gently but surely. If you think the finished mixture is too sticky to be rolled out, add more flour, but do so sparingly, as too much will make the dough tough.

Halve the dough, form into fat disks, wrap each in plastic wrap and rest in the refrigerator for at least an hour.

Sprinkle a suitable surface with flour, place a disk of dough (not taking out the other half until you've finished with the first) on top of it and sprinkle a little more flour on top of that. Then roll it out to a thickness of about half an inch. This dough is such a dream to work that it makes this a rather pleasurable activity.

Cut into shapes, dipping the cutter into flour as you go, and place the cut-out cookies a little apart on the baking sheets.

Bake for 8–12 minutes, by which time they will be lightly golden around the edges but otherwise still quite pale. Cool on a rack—they do firm up when they're cold—and continue with the rest of the dough.

It's hard to be accurate about the number of cookies you'll get out of this mixture without knowing what cutters you'll be using, but in general I reckon on making 60 cookies out of these quantities.

As for the icing: who am I to interfere with the artist within you? All I would do is urge you to try and get hold of the color pastes that come in little tubs (and can be bought from specialized cake shops and increasingly, though not with such an expansive range, in supermarkets) rather than use those little bottles of liquid food coloring. The choice of colors is better, for one thing, and they don't water down the icing when you add them.

NOTES

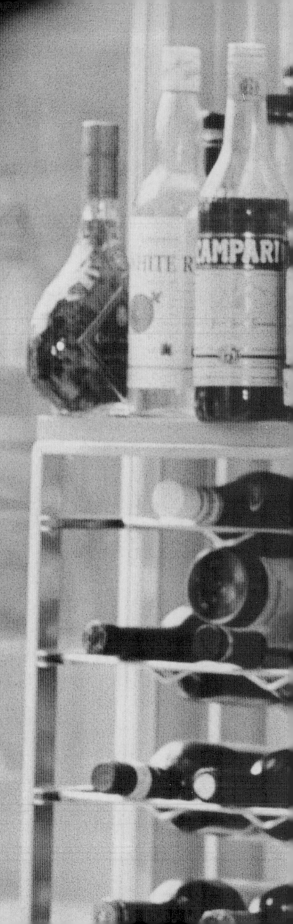

CHAPTER SIX

TRASHY

Enjoying food, enjoying eating, isn't about graduating with honors from the Good Taste University. I'm not interested in pleasing food snobs or purists, or in eating just one type of food. Yes, I want whatever I do eat to be good, but there is surely a place—and in my heart a very fond one—for a bit of kitsch in the kitchen.

HAM IN COCA-COLA

This recipe is from my first book, *How to Eat*, with some rejigging (just because it's not in my nature to leave completely alone), and I don't apologize for reproducing, or rather recasting, it because I simply cannot urge you to try this strongly enough. The first time I made it, it was, to be frank, really just out of amused interest. I'd heard, and read, about this culinary tradition from the Deep South, but wasn't expecting it, in all honesty, to be good. The truth is it's magnificent, and makes converts of anyone who eats it. But, if you think about it, it's not surprising it should work: the sweet, spiky drink just infuses it with the spirit of barbecue. I have to force myself to cook ham any other way now; though often I don't bother with the glaze but just leave it for longer in the bubbling Coke instead.

And the salty, sweet liquor it leaves behind in the pot after it's cooked makes an instant base for the most fabulous black bean soup.

But just one thing before we start: don't even consider using Diet Coke; it's full-sugar or nothing.

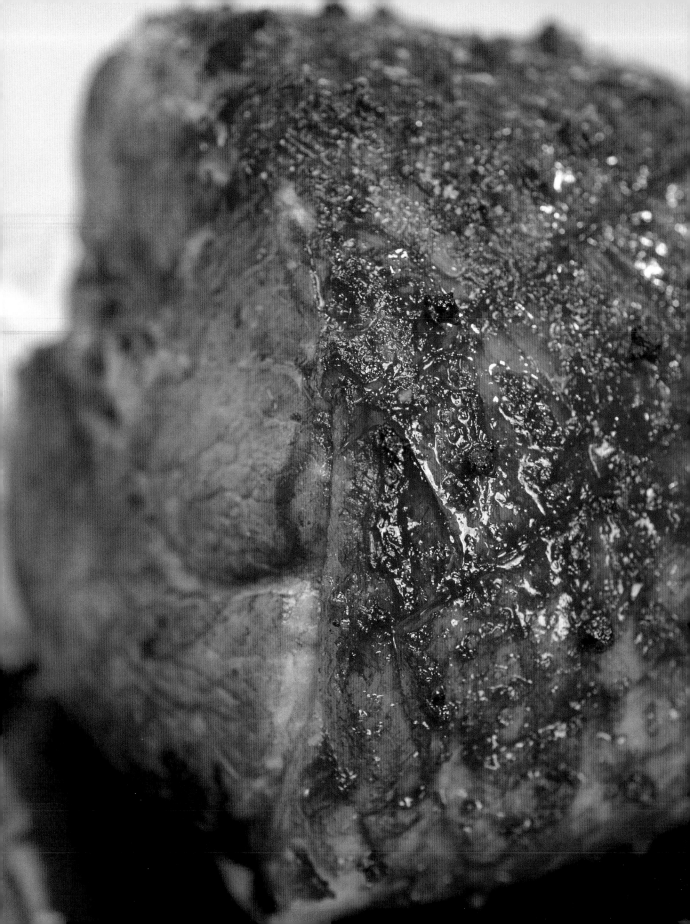

4¼- to 4½-pound bone-in ham
1 onion, peeled and cut in half
2-liter bottle of Coca-Cola

for the glaze:
handful of cloves
1 heaping tablespoon molasses
2 teaspoons English mustard powder
2 tablespoons Demerara or granulated
  brown sugar

If you know that you're dealing with a salty ham, put it in a pan covered with cold water, bring to the boil, then tip into a colander in the sink and start from here; otherwise, put the ham in a pan, skin-side down if it fits like that, add the onion, then pour over the Coke. Bring to the boil, reduce to a good simmer, put the lid on, though not tightly, and cook for just under 2½ hours. If your joint is larger or smaller, work out timing by reckoning on an hour for every 2 pounds, remembering that it's going to get a quick blast in the oven later. But do take into account that if the ham's been in the refrigerator right up to the moment you cook it, you will have to give it a good 15 minutes or so extra so that the interior is properly cooked.

Meanwhile, preheat the oven to 500°F.

When the ham's had its time, take it out of the pan (but do *not* throw away the cooking liquid) and let cool a little for ease of handling. (Indeed, you can let it cool completely then finish off the cooking at some later stage if you want.) Then remove the skin, leaving a thin layer of fat. Score the fat with a sharp knife to make fairly large diamond shapes, and stud each diamond with a clove. Then carefully spread the molasses over the bark-budded skin, taking care not to dislodge the cloves. Gently pat the mustard and sugar onto the sticky fat. Cook in a foil-lined roasting pan for approximately 10 minutes or until the glaze is burnished and bubbly.

Should you want to do the braising stage in advance and then let the ham cool, clove and glaze it and give it 30–40 minutes, from room temperature, at 350°F, turning up the heat toward the end if you think it needs it.

This is seriously fabulous with anything, but the eggily golden Sweet Corn Pudding that follows is perfect: ham and eggs Southern style.

Serves 8.

SWEET CORN PUDDING

This isn't pudding as in dessert, but as in rich, heavy, airless soufflé. I suppose there's nothing to stop you separating the eggs, whisking the whites and turning this into a lighter, frothier affair, but there is most definitely no need. This is easy to make, toothsome and comforting to eat, and I have Gabbie de Jersey to thank for it.

There's something particularly gratifying in specifying a can of cream-style sweet corn in a recipe, but then I have a great sentimental affection for it. When I was about twelve, it was my idea of gastronomic heaven. And needless to say, children love this: thrown together, in smaller quantities to be sure, and paired with some slices of deli ham, it makes for a simple, stress-free supper, one that's likely to be eaten, not pushed whiningly to the side of the plate.

5 eggs

18 ounces (about 2¼ cups) canned sweet corn, drained

14 ounces (about 1¾ cups) canned creamed corn

1⅓ cups whole milk

1⅓ cups heavy cream

generous ⅓ cup all-purpose flour

½ teaspoon baking powder

½ teaspoon salt

Preheat the oven to 375°F and butter an ovenproof dish—and I use my old, scuffed Pyrex one, which measures 12 x 10 inches.

Whisk the eggs in a large bowl, and then add, beating unenergetically, all the other ingredients. Pour into the buttered dish and cook for about an hour, by which time it should have set within and puffed up slightly on the top.

Serves 8.

SOUTH BEACH BLACK BEAN SOUP

This soup bears the name of one in my earlier book, *How to Eat*, but is very different in composition. There are fewer ingredients in it and fewer demands on the cook who makes it. But how could I lose such a title—in this chapter of all places?

The point about this is that it provides a way of using up the sweet, dark liquor that the Coke-cooked ham on page 124 has left behind. I know I'm extravagant, but as I'm so fond of intoning, I'm never wasteful, and this is a rewarding way of satisfying my need to use up every last thing in the kitchen. It's not as if you need to make the soup right away; by all means freeze the stock for future soups if you want. In terms of flavor, I dare say it could be used for a variety of soups, but there is an aesthetic factor to be considered—which isn't the same thing as being queeny about presentation. The point about black beans is that they're black: what do they care about the color of the stock they're simmered in? If anything, the sludgy darkness of this liquid enhances their muddy glory.

I never soak black beans: just make sure that when you cook them they get their 10 toxin-destroying minutes of vociferous boiling and you're off.

About 3 cups (18 ounces) dried black beans
Coca-Cola ham stock from earlier recipe plus water if needed
juice of ½ lime
1 teaspoon ground cumin
1 teaspoon ground coriander

to serve:
sour cream
fresh cilantro, chopped
lime wedges

Cook the black beans in enough Coca-Cola ham stock and water, if needed, to cover by about 2 inches until they're tender. Let the liquid first come to a boil and then reduce the heat to low and cook, partially covered, for 1 to 1½ hours. Remove about 3 ladles of the soup to a blender, add the lime juice and ground spices, blitz to a muddy purée and stir this back into the pan of soup. And that's it.

Swirl some sour cream, as you please, into the bowls of soup as you ladle them out and sprinkle with freshly chopped cilantro. Plonk the lime wedges onto the table and let people squeeze the sharp juice into this dense, sweet soup as they eat.

Serves 8.

CORNBREAD-ON-THE-COB

The golden sweetness of cornbread goes perfectly with the dark intensity of the black bean soup. Now, you can make cornbread in loaf, square or muffin pans, but I love the cornbread that comes in cornsticks—made by cooking the mixture in cast-iron molds that resemble folk art themselves, to give the nubbly form of corn-on-the-cob. There's something about making food in funny shapes, however soberly compelling the taste, that just has "trashy" all over it, and is very gratifying, too, sometimes. You can buy these sorts of molds; mine come from the Broadway Panhandler in New York (a shop with stock as good as its name), which I understandably cherish.

Get some if you can, especially if you've got children, to whom, though not exclusively, they appeal. And eat these golden miniature maize breads with stews, with the black bean soup, with fried eggs and bacon, or just as they are, for breakfast.

vegetable shortening for greasing cornsticks, or butter for pans
1 cup plus 2 tablespoons fine cornmeal (or polenta: same difference really)
3/4 cup all-purpose flour
2 tablespoons sugar
fat pinch of salt

1 tablespoon baking powder
1 cup plus 2 tablespoons whole milk
1 egg
3 tablespoons unsalted butter, melted and cooled

Preheat the oven to 400°F, then grease the cornstick molds with melted vegetable shortening. Those sadly lacking in the cornstick-mold department should grease a square 8-inch baking pan or 12-cup muffin pan with butter (if you're not using paper baking cups).

Mix the cornmeal, flour, sugar, salt and baking powder in a large bowl. In a measuring cup beat together the milk, egg and cooled, melted butter. Then pour the wet ingredients into the dry, stirring with a wooden spoon until just combined. Don't worry in the slightest about the odd lump. Pour into the greased molds and bake for 12–15 minutes for the cornsticks or 20–25 minutes for the square or muffin pans. When ready, the cornbread should be just pulling away from the sides.

Cut the square, if using, into smaller, chunky squares or tip out the cornsticks or muffins and eat warm. And these cornsticks, swabbed with butter as if you really were eating corn-on-the-cob, are God's way of telling you that greed really is good.

Makes 18 cornsticks, 12 muffins or 9 squares of cornbread.

WATERMELON DAIQUIRI

The trashy cook should not be stoveside too long without a drink in hand. And preferably this drink. You don't have to go overboard with the postmodern, anxiously ironic bit: this is ambrosia for even the good-taste gods.

But if on the other hand you're concerned that commendation might detract from its vulgar charm, just make it and drink it, wearing mules to match.

The watermelon doesn't come frozen, by the way, engaging thought though that is: just buy it, slice it, chunk it, stuff it into suitable bags and stash them vibrantly in the freezer.

⅓ cup (or to taste) light rum
juice of 1 good-sized lime
1 heaping tablespoon confectioners'
  sugar

approx. 10 2-inch cubes of frozen
  watermelon

Put all the above ingredients in a blender and blitz to a pinkly foamy purée. Pour into two waiting margarita glasses—and tip back, bangles jangling.

Serves 2.

SOUTHERN-STYLE CHICKEN

There's something about frying, especially in vegetable shortening and in such Rosanne-like quantities, that is so refreshingly unchic. But I assure you there's no element of let's-go-slumming smuggery about the inclusion of this recipe here, for all the glee I take in the gorgeously garish wrapper in which my vegetable shortening of choice comes. This is exceptionally good, a taste sensation and textural heaven; bite into it and savor a finely balanced contrast—tender, poached meat within, crisp coating seared onto it—that the great names of the old Nouvelle Cuisine could only dream of.

Southern cooks use buttermilk for steeping, and fry their soak-softened meat from raw. I use ordinary milk, and poach the chicken in it before frying. Whether this makes it authentically Southern-fried chicken I wouldn't like to say, but regard this as *homage* rather than imitation.

2 chicken drumsticks, skin on
2 chicken thigh portions, skin on, bone in
3–4 cups whole milk
1 tablespoon plus 1 teaspoon salt

¾ cup all-purpose flour
1 teaspoon cayenne pepper
1 egg, beaten
2¼ cups solid vegetable shortening for frying

Put the chicken pieces in a dish into which they fit snugly. Pour over the milk to cover and sprinkle with the tablespoon of salt. Dibble with your fingers to mix in. Cover with plastic wrap and leave in the refrigerator for a few hours or overnight. (You don't absolutely have to do this, but it will help tenderize the meat.)

Tip the contents of the dish into a pan with a lid and bring to the boil, turning it down to simmer until the chicken pieces are entirely cooked through. The pan will look like a horrible, clumpy, curdy mess but don't be put off—it makes the chicken taste wonderful later, which is what matters. Also it's hard to fry chicken really well (or I find it so) from raw, as the skin tends to burn before the meat's cooked at the bone. This is simply my way of resolving this.

Remove the chicken pieces to a rack and let cool; they don't need to be cold, but you don't want them still steamy. Put the flour, cayenne and teaspoon of salt into a plastic bag, shake all the pieces of chicken in it one by one, then dip them into the egg, then into the flour again.

Leave to dry on the rack for about 15 minutes. Heat the great white slab of vegetable shortening in a frying pan until it's nearly at smoking point. Don't worry about using so much: the more fat and the hotter it is, the less the food you're cooking absorbs. So, untroubled, lower in the chicken pieces and cook for a minute or so each side—just long enough for the skin to crisp and turn a rich golden brown.

Eat hot, straight from the pan, with potato chips and a green salad—or, believe it or not, cold. These gold-and-bronzed beauties make killer picnic food.

Serves 2–4.

ELVIS PRESLEY'S FRIED PEANUT BUTTER
AND BANANA SANDWICH

Let's not mess around: you want trashy, I'll give you trashy—I'll give you the King. This recipe, for want of a better word, comes from a rhinestone gem of a cookbook, *Are You Hungry Tonight?*, a collection of Elvis's favorite foodstuffs bought on a visit to Graceland many years back, prized ever since and a delight from cover to cover. Even my most recent addition to a library already bursting with bad-taste titles, *Liberace Cooks!*, can't lose him his crown.

You'd think, wouldn't you, that smearing a couple of slabs of white bread with peanut butter and mashed banana, sandwiching the lot bulgingly together and then frying it in butter, would be at best revolting. But that's where you'd be wrong. I have no particular fondness for peanut butter, or bananas for that matter, and a downright shuddering aversion to eating them cooked, but what a genius that man was. This sandwich is a wondrous thing, gloriously exemplifying what cooking is all about: the whole is so much intriguingly, confoundingly more than the sum of its parts. It really works. I wouldn't turn one down now at any time, although, true to form, there is a certain kamikaze calorie-intake involved not always to be calmly countenanced—but for a hangover, to combat seediness and restore the fragmenting self, it's particular perfection: it doesn't merely sustain, it resuscitates.

Believe it or not, the quantities below appear in edited, attenuated form. I honor the King but I can't be him.

1 small ripe banana
2 slices white bread

2 scant tablespoons creamy peanut butter
2 tablespoons butter

Mash or slice the banana.

Lightly toast the bread, and then spread the peanut butter on one piece and the banana on the other. Sandwich together, then fry in the butter, turning once, until each side is golden brown. Remove to a plate, cut the sandwich carefully in half on the diagonal and eat.

Serves 1.

DEEP-FRIED CANDY BARS WITH PINEAPPLE

Or Glasgow meets the Caribbean. Francis MacNeil, the lighting assistant on my television series, told me about the joys of deep-fried coconut-filled chocolate bars (far in excess, I should say, of the more familiar regional dish of deep-fried Milky Ways), and since I had people coming for dinner at the end of that week, I just had to try it. I should say that I offered it as a perfectly serious dessert—more or less—after a starter of tuna with ginger, soy and rice vinegar, a take on the salmon recipe on page 178 and the Thai Seafood Curry on page 66: it was a triumph.

The pineapple cuts across the sticky sweetness of the fritters and turns it into a dessert rather than a funny turn. Besides, the combination of coconut and pineapple is a time-honored one. You might consider putting a bottle of good rum on the table for people to drink alongside, too.

As for the batter: I find the combination of self-rising flour and soda water produces the lightest effect possible.

And since then, I have been inspired to move on to deep-fried Cadbury's Creme Eggs (a must for Easter) and deep-fried Dime Bars. There's no stopping me now . . .

approx. 2 quarts sunflower or other oil for deep frying	**1 cup self-rising flour**
1 ripe pineapple	**about 1 cup soda water**
	8 fun-sized Mounds bars

Heat the oil in a deep-fat fryer to maximum heat.

Cut the top and bottom off the pineapple, and then quarter it vertically. Trim the woody core off each segment, and then lay it skin-side down, and slice the flesh in half lengthwise, stopping when you feel the skin. Then cut it across into slices and run the knife between the flesh of the fruit and the outer husk. The pineapple pieces should then come away easily. Squeeze the outer skin of the pineapple over the cut fruit to get every last bit of juice.

Measure the flour into a bowl, and whisk in ¾ cup of the soda water to make the batter, adding the rest of the water if the consistency is still too thick: you want this just thick enough to adhere easily. The best way to check is to turn a Mounds bar in it: if the batter sticks well enough, it's fine. I just use my fingers for this, but tongs work well, too.

Plunge the batter-blanketed Mounds in the hot oil and fry for about 3 minutes until the batter's puffed and golden. Remove to pieces of paper towel to absorb excess grease, then pile up on a plate to sit on the table alongside the cut-up pineapple.

CHOCOLATE-LIME CHEESECAKE

Perhaps it is eccentric to wait for the last recipe in the chapter before pausing to explain what it is that makes any food trashy, as far as my purposes here are concerned, but nothing exemplifies it better than this cheesecake. Right then: you should know I start from the premise—and this is resolutely the case with all the recipes here—that, all campiness aside, it has to be good, better than good: it can taste surprisingly elegant or prejudice-challengingly seductive, but the one thing it mustn't taste like is a joke.

If that's understood, we can move on. Trashy food, in its platonic ideal, should contain at least one brand-name product. Here we have the Philadelphia cream cheese leading. Next, it should use a low-rent ingredient, one that gastro-snobs would never normally even consider keeping in the house: may I introduce you to chocolate wafer cookies? (Yes, I like them too, but we're talking culinary status-queens here, the pose of the label-conscious purist.) Finally, in its loftiest incarnation, it should seek to evoke some food or food-related substance that is industrially produced, not naturally occurring. Here, my inspiration for the cheesecake was a sweet—those chocolate limes I ate in my childhood.

That the base is rich and dark and perfectly counters the light, tender cream-cheese custard above it, itself kept all the more delicately smooth by being baked in a water bath (and this is easy: don't let a bit of wrapping in foil and boiling a kettle put you off before you start) and made intensely, fragrantly sharp by having the juice of four uncompromisingly sour limes squeezed into it, takes us back to the beginning. Trashy is a state of mind, a game of mood: the food itself deserves, *demands*, to be served and eaten—unsmirkingly, unapologetically and with voluptuous and exquisite pleasure.

7 ounces chocolate wafer cookies

1/3 cup unsalted butter

1 1/2 pounds Philadelphia cream cheese

1 cup sugar

4 whole eggs

2 yolks

juice of 4 small limes (approx. 3/4 cup)

8-inch springform cake pan

aluminum foil

Place a large overlapping piece of foil over the bottom of the springform pan, and then insert the pan ring over it. Fold the foil up around the sides of the pan and place the whole thing on a second piece of foil, also folding it and pressing it securely up around the pan so that you have a water-tight covering. Actually, I sometimes find some water dribbles out from this supposedly secure casing on unwrapping, but it doesn't seem—as long as you unwrap the outer layer straightaway—to cause any sogginess.

Process the cookies until they are like crumbs, then add the butter and pulse again. Line the bottom of the springform pan, pressing the cookies in with your hands or the back of a spoon. Put the pan in the refrigerator to set, and preheat the oven to 350°F.

Beat the cream cheese gently until it's smooth, and then add the sugar. Beat in the eggs and egg yolks, then finally the lime juice. Put a full kettle on.

Pour the cream cheese filling onto the chilled cookie base, place the cake pan in a roasting pan and pour hot water from the recently boiled kettle around the foil-wrapped cheesecake to come about halfway up the sides of the springform; don't overfill, as you'll only spill it on the way to the oven. Transfer it as steadily as you can to the oven and cook for 1 hour or so, checking after 50 minutes. It should feel set, but not rigidly so. You want to be able to detect, below the skin, the slightest, sexiest hint of quiver within.

Take the roasting pan out of the oven, then gingerly remove the springform from its water-filled pan, stand it on a rack, peel off the outer layer of foil, tear away the side bits of the first layer of foil and leave to cool. When the cheesecake's cooled down completely, place it in the refrigerator and leave it there till 20 minutes or so before you want to eat it.

Transfer to the plate you're going to serve it on (it will need to be one without a lip, or a cakestand) and unclip. The underneath bit of the first layer of foil, along with the base of the pan, are going to have to stay in place, unless you like living really dangerously. I don't mind a bit of risk in the kitchen, but fiddling about with something as desirably lacking in solidity as this dreamlike cheesecake is beyond even my clumsily impatient foolhardiness.

It makes life easier if, when you cut it, you heat the knife and cake slicer (and I find I need to use both, the one to cut, the other to lift up and ferry slice to waiting plate) under a very hot tap first.

Serves 8.

NOTES

NOTES

CHAPTER SEVEN

LEGACY

The way I cook, more than what I cook, is so much a product of the way my mother cooked before me, and most of what I feel about food comes from my family. Every time I pick up a pan I am drawing on what I inherited—cooking is nothing if not about temperament and habit—but there are some special dishes that I either ate as a child or that come from the family kitchen. These have a special significance for me that I want to keep alive and pass on.

ITALIAN SAUSAGES WITH LENTILS

My mother used English sausages mostly, and those flat, sludgy lentils (Puy lentils weren't so easily available then), but this is at its best made with highly flavored Italian sausages (I love the ones tagged "Genovese," deep with garlic and basil) and either French Puy lentils or the similar Italian ones from Umbria.

This isn't about fancifying a down-home dish: it's about doing what feels right and responding to what's available; in short, it's about cooking.

This, incidentally, is what Italians serve traditionally on New Year's Day; the coin-shaped lentils symbolize the prosperity that is hoped for over the coming year, much as Jewish tradition uses honey richly for the Rosh Hashanah meal to represent the wish for a sweet and happy life for the year ahead.

3–4 tablespoons olive oil (not extra-virgin)
1 onion, finely chopped
sprinkling of salt
About 2³⁄₄ cups (18 ounces) dried Puy lentils

1 fat clove garlic, squished with the flat side of a knife, and skin removed
8 Italian sausage links
¹⁄₃ cup plus 1 tablespoon red wine
¹⁄₄ cup water
flat-leaf parsley for sprinkling

To cook the lentils, put 2–3 tablespoons of the oil into a good-sized saucepan (and one that has a lid that fits) on the heat and when it's warm add the chopped onion. Sprinkle with salt (which helps prevent its browning) and cook over a low to medium heat till soft (about 5 minutes). Add the lentils, stir well and then cover generously with cold water. Bring to the boil, then cover and let simmer gently for half an hour or so until cooked and most, if not all, the liquid's absorbed. I don't add salt at this stage since the sauce provided by the sausages later (and which will be poured over the lentils) will be pretty salty itself. So, wait and taste. And remember, you can of course cook the lentils in advance.

Anyway, when either the lentils are nearly ready or you're about to reheat them, put a heavy-based frying pan on the burner, cover with a film of oil and add the bruised garlic. Cook for a few minutes then add and brown the sausages. When the sausages are brown on both sides—which won't take more than 5 minutes or so—throw in the wine and water and let bubble up. Cover the pan, either with a lid or aluminum foil, and cook for about 15 minutes. Using a fork, mash the now-soft garlic into the sauce and taste for seasoning, adding a little more water if it's too strong.

Remove the lentils to a shallowish bowl or dish (I evacuate the sausages from their cooking pan, plonk the lentils in, then proceed) then cover with the sausages and their garlicky, winey gravy. Sprinkle over some flat-leaf parsley.

Serves 4.

SOFT-BOILED EGGS WITH ASPARAGUS SOLDIERS

No, we didn't eat this for breakfast when I was a child, so keep calm. It's just that I remember eating asparagus like this, dipped into oily-yolked soft-boiled eggs or pronged into the soft, bulging, yellow belly of a fried one (in which case, it becomes Asparagus Holstein). It's a good way of making the expensive bundles of early spring asparagus go further, and besides, the richness of the flowing, viscous yolk provides the best and simplest sauce for the bud-tipped grass. Consider serving this as a starter; go further, too, if you like and provide plates of puce-pink salty-sweet prosciutto, the slices to be used as edible damask napkins with which to wrap and hold the juicy green stems.

1 bunch of asparagus   **Maldon or other sea salt**
4 eggs at room temperature

Cut the woody ends off the asparagus, and cook it in a shallow saucepan of boiling water until it's tender but still has some bite—about 5 minutes. Then drain them and keep them warm while you cook the eggs.

In a saucepan, bring some water to the boil into which you have dropped a matchstick; according to my Aunt Frieda this stops the white from billowing out into the pan should the egg crack while cooking. Am I going to promise this works? Well, all families have their folklore.

Lower the eggs into the water and cook them at a steady boil for about 4 minutes. Take them out of the water and immediately slice the top off each one; the yolk should still be runny enough to dip the asparagus spears in.

Make sure there's salt on the table for sprinkling into the almost aggressive blandness of the egg and spear, as you eat, with the warm asparagus.

Serves 4.

WHITEBAIT

I'd almost forgotten about whitebait until I saw it in the fishmonger's recently, and—in honor of my new(ish) deep-fat fryer—bought it and took it home to cook. When I was a child, this was *the* restaurant starter; now it seems to have disappeared from the menu altogether. I didn't eat it then, but my father and sister, Thomasina, always ordered it, and it is partly in her memory, and with the wish that she was still here to eat it, that I present it to you now.

It is so unfamiliar now that some of you may need me to tell you what whitebait is, or are. Whitebait is just small fish, indeed the original "small fry," and it's the size rather than the genus that's significant. Generally, it refers to very young herring or sprats, and these are deep-fried and eaten whole. The fish comes, frozen now, in bags, which is straightforward enough. The cooking is minimal: the whitebait are dredged in flour (deviled whitebait being tossed in flour heavily dusted with cayenne), plunged into hot fat, piled on a plate and served with deep-fried parsley, a squeeze of lemon (muslin-covered if we're being traditional here) and brown bread and butter. Of course, the parsley in question is the old, curly kind, which has long been awaiting rehabilitation.

vegetable oil for frying
18 ounces whitebait
½ cup flour
salt and pepper

1 bunch curly parsley
Maldon or other sea salt
lemons for serving

Heat the oil for frying in a deep-fat fryer to about 375°F.

Put the whitebait and seasoned flour into a plastic bag, and toss everything around to coat the fish.

Shake off the excess flour by turning out the whole bag into a metal sieve, and then plunge the little fishes into the oil. Cook for about 3 minutes or until they look crispy and tempting—though I can see that for a squeamish generation, the idea of eating baby fish, whole, might not tempt. How wrong they are, if that's the case.

Turn them out onto paper towels, and while the fish are losing any excess oil (we want desirable crunch) throw in a small handful of parsley to deep-fry; watch out, it will spit. (A splatter guard is useful. Not charming, but useful.) When it has turned a very dark green, drain it and serve it with the whitebait, well sprinkled with sea salt and surrounded with lemon wedges.

Serves 2 as a main course or 4 as a starter.

LIPTAUER

What did I get myself into, deciding to put this here? It sounds, or will once I explain it, so unlikely, so culinarily yesteryear. But if we're talking family favorites I couldn't leave it out. Liptauer was *the* deli-counter delicacy of my childhood, and another eating-item I'd all but forgotten about. But something made me remember it and, from taste-memory and some notes from the kitchen book inherited by my friend Olivia from her mother, I tried my hand at making it myself, and I can confidently and categorically state that it's not some sentimental yearning that makes me now want to see its comeback. You don't need to go in for the retro-molding here, just mix the ingredients and plonk them in a bowl if you like: but whatever, this glorious, cream cheese, caper, caraway seed and paprika combination, spread over sour black bread or—if you don't have the genetic taste for it—over slices of any dark or brown bread, which you can get from the supermarket, is rhapsodically unbeatable.

18 ounces cream cheese	**2 teaspoons caraway seeds**
2¼ cups cottage cheese	**2 teaspoons French mustard**
4–5 tablespoons capers	**1-quart mold or bowl**
8 cornichons, chopped	
3 teaspoons paprika	***for drizzling over:***
pinch of salt	**1–2 tablespoons flavorless vegetable oil**
good grating of black pepper	**fat pinch of paprika**

Beat the two cheeses together until they are smooth, and then add all the other ingredients. Mix everything together well, and then turn into a small bowl with a capacity of approximately 1 quart, lined with plastic wrap for easier unmolding later. Smooth the top with a spatula and cover with the overhanging plastic wrap. Place it in the refrigerator to set. I put a couple of cans on top to press it down, but I don't feel it's crucial. I think it's because my mother was always putting pâtés and suchlike in the refrigerator with weights on.

When it has become cold enough to turn out—a few hours should do it—unwrap the folded-over plastic wrap on top, place a plate over the now uncovered bowl, turn it the other way out and unmold. Pull the plastic wrap off and drizzle over a rust-red ooze, made by mixing the oil with a pinch of paprika.

Serve this with bread or poppy-seed-sprinkled bagels, gherkins and, if you like, some chopped red onions.

GRANNY LAWSON'S LUNCH DISH

When my paternal grandmother died recently, I got all her old, battered cookery notebooks, and this is a recipe from one of them. In truth, I don't remember her cooking it ever, but then she took the decision relatively early on in my life that she got vertigo in the kitchen and therefore, in the interest of health you understand, cooked rarely. But I love these sorts of domestic diaries, half-filled with recipes torn out from papers, the rest a handwritten mixture of tips passed on by friends or accounts of lunches served to them. Cooking isn't just about ingredients, weights and measures: it's social history, personal history.

I love, too, the simplicity of its name as it appears in my grandmother's hand—just "lunch dish." And yes, I won't deny it has a retro-appeal—the chopped hard-boiled eggs and olives in the pie somehow even now convey the sense of adventurousness that a fifties' housewife would have had in making this—but it tastes fabulously good, hot or cold.

In cooking this, I altered things as I went along. For example, I have my way of making pastry (freezing the fat and flour together for 10 minutes before rubbing them in) and prefer to use Italian 00 or pasta flour, which makes for a helpfully elastic dough, but that's part of what makes cooking alive. (Interestingly, though, the olive oil specified is not a contemporary addition but my grandmother's untampered-with injunction.) It has to be an improvisational rather than a formulaic activity. As with everything that matters in life, if it isn't honest, it's nothing.

If pastry seems daunting to you, then this is a good place to start, because it's a rough, ramshackle square of a thing: no fancy tins, no fancy techniques.

for the pastry:
1²/₃ cups all-purpose flour, preferably Italian 00
scant ¹/₄ cup solid vegetable shortening
6 tablespoons cold, unsalted butter
approx. 4 tablespoons chilled, lightly salted water
1 egg beaten with pinch of salt for brushing

2–3 (about 12 ounces) tomatoes or same amount of drained, chopped, canned ones
2 small onions
2 eggs, hard-boiled
4 ounces pitted black olives
2 tablespoons olive oil, not extra-virgin
9 ounces organic ground beef
fat pinch allspice
salt and pepper

To make the pastry, measure the flour into a dish that will fit into the freezer (it doesn't need to have a lid) and cut the shortening and butter into small—approximately ¹/₂-inch—dice and toss them in the flour. Put in the freezer for 10 minutes.

I tend to make pastry in my KitchenAid, but a processor's fine too. In whatever

contraption—fitted with the flat paddle in the one, with the double-bladed knife in the other—mix until you have a mixture that resembles coarse uncooked oatmeal. Now, dribble in the chilled salted water, slowly, with the motor still running, until the dough looks as if it's about to cohere, but stopping short of its actually clumping totally. Turn out of the processor (though you could still do this in the bowl of the mixer) and squidge together with your hands until all the pastry forms a cohesive ball. Dribble in a little more water if you feel it needs it. Divide into two pieces of equal size and form into fat disks. Cover with plastic wrap and leave in the refrigerator for 20 minutes. And this can be done a good day or two in advance if it helps.

Preheat the oven to 400°F.

Put the tomatoes in a bowl, cover with boiling water from the kettle and leave for 5 minutes. Drain, run under the cold tap, then peel, seed and chop roughly (or use canned tomatoes, chopped and drained). Peel and chop the onions, hard-boiled eggs and olives, too.

In a large frying pan over medium heat, warm the oil. Cook the chopped onions until softened and beginning to color, turning the flame down to low if they look as if they're sticking. Turn the heat back to medium and add the chopped tomatoes and cook, stirring for a minute or so before adding the beef. Stir well, breaking up the clumps of

meat with your wooden spoon as you go, then, when the meat's browned, stir in the chopped eggs and olives and season with the allspice and salt and pepper. Cook over gentle heat for about 20 minutes, stirring occasionally.

Get a baking sheet out, and flour a surface and rolling pin. Remove the pastry from the refrigerator and roll out one of the disks until you have a thin, but not exaggeratedly so, rough square that will fit on the baking sheet, then place it on the sheet. Now roll out the second disk and leave it there while you cover the layer on the sheet with the ground beef mixture, leaving a margin of about 1 inch all around. With a bit of cold water and your fingers, dampen this edge. Place the second square of pastry on top and press the edges together to seal. Now, roll these edges back on themselves once or twice, then get a fork and press it, the tines curved-side down, against this rolled border. Prong the top of the pastry to make air holes and then beat the egg with a generous sprinkling of salt and brush the top and edges of the pie with it to glaze.

Put it in the oven for 20 minutes, by which time the pastry will be golden and cooked. Slice it into fat oblongs and eat warm with a vegetable or salad, or cold, wrapped in a napkin and without ceremony or cutlery.

Serves 6.

MY GRANDMOTHER'S GINGER-JAM
BREAD AND BUTTER PUDDING

This recipe comes from my maternal grandmother's recipe folder, a wonderfully retro piece of design, circa late sixties, early seventies. Bread and butter pudding has, I know, gone from stodgy disparagement to fashionable rehabilitation and back to not-that-again clichédom, but I am not prepared to let any of that bother me.

This version uses brown bread rather than white, and between the buttery sandwiches is heaped chunky-hot ginger jam, sometimes sold as ginger marmalade, but most usually, if quaintly, as ginger conserve; on top is sprinkled Demerara sugar mixed with aromatically warm ground ginger, the spice of the old-fashioned English kitchen.

My grandmother, more austerely, used milk; I go for mostly cream: nothing creates so well that tender-bellied swell of softly set custard.

6 tablespoons unsalted butter

⅓ cup golden raisins

3 tablespoons dark rum

10 slices brown bread

approx. 10 tablespoons ginger conserve or marmalade

4 egg yolks

1 egg

3 tablespoons sugar

2¼ cups heavy cream

¾ cup plus 2 tablespoons whole milk

1 teaspoon ground ginger

2 tablespoons Demerara or granulated brown sugar

Preheat the oven to 350°F.

Grease a pudding dish or shallow baking dish with a capacity of about 1½ quarts with some of the butter.

Put the raisins in a small bowl, pour the rum over and microwave them for 1 minute, then leave them to stand. This is a good way to soak them quickly but juicily.

Make sandwiches with the brown bread, butter and ginger jam (2 tablespoonfuls in each sandwich); you should have some butter left over to smear on the top later. Now cut the sandwiches in half into triangles and arrange them evenly along the middle of the dish. I put one in the dish with the point of the sandwich upward then one with flat-side uppermost, then with point-side uppermost and so on, then squeeze a sandwich-triangle down each side—but you do as you please. Sprinkle over the raisins and unabsorbed rum that remains in the bowl.

Whisk the egg yolks and egg together with the sugar, and pour in the cream and milk. Pour this over the triangles of bread and leave them to soak up the liquid for about 10 minutes, by which time the pudding is ready to go into the oven. Smear the bread crusts that are poking out of the custard with the soft butter, mix the ground ginger and Demerara sugar together and sprinkle this mixture on your buttered crusts and then lightly over the rest of the pudding.

Sit the pudding dish on a baking sheet and put in the oven to cook for about 45 minutes or until the custard has set and puffed up slightly. Remove, let sit for 10 minutes—by which time the puffiness will have deflated somewhat—and spoon out into bowls, putting a pitcher of custard, should you so wish, on the table to be served alongside.

Serves 6.

CUSTARD

If you are going to eat this sort of pudding, it can't hurt to know how to make the custard to go with it. It is useful to know that you need 1 egg yolk for each ½ cup of milk or cream. It's harder to be precise about the sugar, which depends on your taste, what you're eating the custard with and whether it's going to be hot or cold.

**1 vanilla bean or 1 teaspoon vanilla
  extract
2½ cups light cream or half-and half**

**5 large egg yolks
1 generous tablespoon sugar**

Half-fill the sink with cold water.

If you've got a vanilla bean, cut it lengthwise so that the seeds will be released, and heat it in a pan with the cream till nearly boiling. Take off the heat, cover and leave to steep for 20 minutes. If you're not using a bean, put the cream and vanilla extract on the heat, and beat the egg yolks and sugar together in a bowl. When the cream's warm, pour it over the sweet yolks, beating all the while. Pour the uncooked custard back into the rinsed-out and dried pan and cook over a medium heat, stirring constantly, until the custard's thickened. Ten minutes should do it, unless you're being very timorous and leaving the flame too low. When the custard's thickened, plunge the pan into the cold water in the sink and whisk it for a minute or so. You can eat it straight away, or if you want to make it in advance, reheat later in a bowl over a pan of simmering water.

Serves 4.

CHOCOLATE-CHESTNUT REFRIGERATOR CAKE

This is another of my maternal grandmother's recipes and in truth reminds me much more of her than the bread and butter pudding. I've changed it a bit, not least substituting dark rum for her juice and zest of an orange and a slug or two of Grand Marnier. It's not that I didn't like her version, but it was just a bit too much like a homespun Terry's chocolate orange for comfort. You do as you please.

This is very much a period offering: from a time of refrigerated cooked loaves of things, sliced at dinner parties and served with dainty fruit salads (my grandmother suggested some sliced oranges here, which is of a piece), but it nevertheless resolutely deserves a place on the contemporary table. It's incredibly easy to make, and dangerously compelling to eat, one of those desserts about which everyone says "it's very rich" before going on to third helpings.

I think it needs a smooth, sour blob of crème fraîche alongside: it *is* sweet; but the crystallized violets you see adorning the slice opposite are just a sentimental touch. My grandmother loved them, as did my mother; they are, as it happens, the traditional sprinkling accompaniment to monte bianco, that gunge-heavy mixture of cream, chocolate, rum and chestnut purée that—more free-form, less prinked—my mother went in for.

18 ounces canned sweetened chestnut purée	*to serve:*
3/4 cup soft, unsalted butter	**crystallized violets**
11 ounces bittersweet chocolate, minimum 70% cocoa solids	**crème fraîche**
3 tablespoons dark rum	

Beat the purée in a bowl until it's smooth, and then add the butter, beating again to make a well-blended mixture.

Melt the chocolate and let it cool slightly, before adding it to the chestnut and butter in the bowl. Beat in the rum, and spoon the chocolate mixture into an 8½ x 4½-inch loaf tin, lined with plastic wrap, in two batches, making sure the first layer reaches the corners and sides of the bottom of the pan before you smooth over the rest. Wrap the overhanging plastic wrap over the cake so that it is completely covered, and put it in the refrigerator to set for at least four hours, but a day or so in advance if you want.

Don't take the loaf pan out of the refrigerator until you want to eat it, when you just unmold the cake, cut it into thin slices, decorate with the violets and serve with crème fraîche or sour cream.

Makes 10–12 slices.

NOTES

NOTES

CHAPTER EIGHT

SUPPERTIME

There is a way of inviting friends over for dinner without hating them, yourself, the kitchen and the world. Cooking isn't performance art—or shouldn't be. Perhaps it's unrealistic to hope to be a model of serenity throughout, but if you can manage to relax, both the food and the evening will be better. The answer is to cook in a way that doesn't involve huge amounts of effort or time. Ease yourself into a repertoire, make the food welcoming rather than fussy and remember that it's not a test of your worth and acceptability: it's just dinner.

THREE-COURSE DINNER FOR 8

Salmon with ginger, soy and rice vinegar

Redfish with anchovies, thyme and chickpeas; and Egyptian tomato salad

Chocolate pots

I don't, as a rule, always bother with starters, but sometimes you want to go in for a full-fledged dinner party. By that I don't mean that you have to start folding your napkins into fancy shapes or pushing yourself beyond all known gastronomic boundaries. However important food is, it's a part of life, not the whole point of it. A good dinner party is one where people enjoy themselves: the last thing you want is a tense and hallowed silence to descend as you, exhausted, slump some perfect creation on the table, desperate for their approval and admiration. The food—and the drink—are there to give rise to, not upstage, conversation and companionability.

This dinner is eminently do-able without your having to devote the best part of two days to cooking it. Certainly, some of the food is fiddled about with, in a low-effort kind of a way, in advance, but that's just to make life easier on the night.

SALMON WITH GINGER, SOY AND RICE VINEGAR

This is a very easy starter, not least because no cooking is involved at all. All you need to do is mix the first four ingredients, leave them to steep for 10 minutes or so in a large glass measuring cup (longer if it helps), arrange the salmon slices on a couple of large plates and then pour the liquid over before scattering with some finely chopped scallions.

I get the salmon from the fishmonger and ask them to do the fiddly slicing, but otherwise you could use the rag-like salmon fillets some supermarkets sell. And if the idea of raw salmon appalls you, simply flash-fry the fillets, transfer briskly to waiting plates, slice them into wide strips then pour over the gingery juices and serve either as is, still warm, or left to cool to room temperature.

This is also wonderful made with sliver-thin slices of tuna.

¼ **cup soy sauce**
¼ **cup rice vinegar**
1-inch piece of ginger, peeled and grated
  (preferably with a Microplane grater)
1 tablespoon toasted sesame oil
  (optional)

1½ **pounds salmon, preferably organic,**
  sliced as thinly as smoked salmon, or
  as near to that as possible
2–4 scallions, finely sliced

Mix the soy sauce and rice vinegar together and grate in the ginger. If you want to add the sesame oil, do—its aromatic nuttiness adds a rounded mellowness—but salmon is oily enough not to need it, so leave it out if you want something a little more delicately astringent.

Cut the very thin salmon pieces (and I use kitchen scissors for this) into wide strips and arrange them any old how on a couple of plates. Pour over the gingery dressing and scatter the finely sliced scallions on top.

Now was that hard?

REDFISH WITH ANCHOVIES AND THYME

May I make a suggestion? Please don't tell people that the sauce has anchovy in it. What comes through is not fishiness, but a robust, rounded saltiness. So many people have an anti-anchovy prejudice that it's hardly worth the explaining: deception, I've found, is the more sensible route. I use anchovy fillets that have been stored in an olive-oil-filled jar, though a squirt of anchovy paste from a tube is a perfectly respectable substitute.

I make a version of this sauce a lot, with a variety of fish, mostly white; but I ought to tell you it also makes a wonderful sauce for lamb (in which case replace the sherry with red wine). The chickpeas, following, are perfect with the fish or lamb variant, too. And the useful thing is that with all the meaty pulsiness of them, you don't need to bother with potatoes. (And although I've given the recipe for the chickpeas after this, the main course, you do need to get on and cook them first. Be warned.)

Redfish (sometimes called bream) can be replaced with red snapper, ocean perch, sea bream or rockfish. There is a fleshy firmness that makes these chunky fillets stand up well to robust flavors. And the pearl-pink skin, like the flash of a Barbie mermaid's tail, is quite beautiful.

2–4 tablespoons olive oil, plus dribble of	2 anchovy fillets
oil from anchovies	leaves from a few sprigs of thyme
12 fillets of redfish, red snapper, sea	2 tablespoons sherry
bream, ocean perch or rockfish, skin on	1 fat pat unsalted butter (approx. 1
1 clove garlic, minced	tablespoon)

In a large, nonstick frying pan (I use a Woll fish pan here) pour a little olive oil and, when warm, start frying the fish. They won't need much, but keep an eye—some fillets may be thicker than others—and remove to a couple of warm plates, tented with foil, as they're cooked. I think these look best with the pearly pink skin uppermost.

When all the fish fillets are cooked, add a tablespoon of olive oil plus the dribble of anchovy oil to the pan and stir in the minced garlic and the anchovy fillets. Keep stirring with a wooden spoon or spatula and, as the oil warms, the garlic should soften and the anchovies seem to melt into a sauce. Add most of the thyme leaves, then the sherry. After a scant minute's bubbling, replace the wooden spoon in your hand with a wire whisk or a handheld mixer or electric whisk—one of my favorite pieces of equipment—and, off the heat, whisk in the butter. Pour this small amount of viscous sauce over the two plates of fish (this is for flavoring, not coverage), then sprinkle with the few remaining thyme leaves. Serve with the chickpeas and tomato salad. I know this sounds like a lot for 8, but I like to work on making enough for half those present to have second helpings. At any rate, I've found that a good rule of thumb.

CHICKPEAS WITH CHILLI, GARLIC AND THYME

This is the chickpea recipe I return to again and again, with some variation in herbs used; here I've added thyme for aromatic balance with the redfish. If it helps, replace the fresh thyme with dried thyme (as long as it isn't stale and years old) and the fresh red chilli with a dried hot chilli pepper.

There are three things I feel you should know about chickpeas. The first is that they need longer soaking than anyone tells you (24 hours for preference); the second is that they take longer to cook than anyone tells you (1½–2 hours is what you should be reckoning on); and the third is that they will be more buttery, velvety and nuttily tender than you could ever imagine if you make up Anna del Conte's paste of flour, baking soda and salt and add it to the soaking water.

I know long soaking and long cooking make these chickpeas seem a bit of a bother, but nothing's hard, in the first place, and what I find makes life generally easier is that you can cook them in advance. This means that all you really need to do on the night is make the tomato salad, heat up the chickpeas, or turn them in the chilli and so forth, quickly fry the fish and you're off. So in fact, despite lengthy (but not tricky) preparation, this makes for a swiftly and easily assembled drop-dead dinner.

About 3 cups (18 ounces) dried chickpeas

2 tablespoons flour

2 tablespoons salt

2 teaspoons baking soda

1 onion, halved (don't bother to peel it)

6 or so sprigs of thyme

1/4 cup olive oil (not extra-virgin)

Maldon or other sea salt

1 red chilli pepper

1 onion

2 fat cloves garlic

leaves from 4–5 sprigs of thyme

1/4 cup olive oil (not extra-virgin)

good slug extra-virgin olive oil

Soak the chickpeas in enough cold water to cover generously and make a paste up with the flour, salt and baking soda and a little more cold water. Add this to the soaking chickpeas (I just dunk in the bowl I've mixed it up in). Leave for 24 hours.

Drain and thoroughly rinse the chickpeas in a colander under running cold water in the sink. Tip them into a large saucepan, cover abundantly with cold water and add the halved onion, sprigs of thyme and olive oil. Do not salt: at this stage it would make the skins tough. Put on a lid, bring to the boil and let bubble away for an hour and a half. At this stage only may you take off the lid to see how cooked the chickpeas are; you may also now add salt. If they're cooked, you should lower in a measuring cup to remove about 2¼ cups of the cooking water; otherwise keep going until they're ready.

Once you've reserved your chickpea cooking liquid, drain the chickpeas and remove—with tongs for ease—the bits of onion and thyme. This doesn't have to be ruthlessly carried out, but just get rid of any obvious bits. Once cold you can Tupperware the chickpeas, tossing them first in olive oil to prevent drying, until you need them; or else cook them through to the final stage, let them cool and refrigerate them in a covered container or bowl covered with plastic wrap.

Roughly seed and chop the red chilli pepper, peel and chunk the onion, press on the garlic cloves to loosen, then remove the skins, bung everything, along with the thyme leaves, into the processor and blitz to a pulp. In a large, deep frying pan or casserole—whatever suits—pour the oil and, when warm, tip in the pulp from the processor. Sprinkle with salt and cook gently, stirring occasionally, for 5–10 minutes or until soft. Add the chickpeas and turn to coat, then pour in about half the chickpea cooking liquid and bring to a boil. Put on a lid and let cook gently till the chickpeas are hot and soft; you will probably need to remove the lid at the end of cooking to let excess water evaporate. If, however, you run out of liquid before the chickpeas are tender and soused enough, simply add more of the reserved water.

When the chickpeas are ready, turn into a large bowl, or keep in the pan in which you've cooked them, and add extra-virgin olive oil: drizzle then stir and keep going until the chickpeas are glossy but not too thickly slicked. Sprinkle over sea salt and some thyme leaves if you feel like it (and happen to have some scattered anyway over the work surface—you might well at this stage) or leave them simply oiled and salted.

EGYPTIAN TOMATO SALAD

I found this salad in a lovely little book—"a memoir with recipes"—called *Apricots on the Nile*, by Colette Rossant. And although it sounds a lot of bother blanching and peeling the tomatoes, all in fact it involves is leaving the tomatoes for a few minutes in a bowlful of just-boiled water, after which their skins will come off without any trouble. It is worth doing this: the tomatoes will be more seductively tender and the nubbly dressing then permeates them better.

If a shallot is beyond you, use the white parts of two or three scallions.

1 shallot, peeled
1 clove of garlic, peeled
3–4 tablespoons olive oil
salt and pepper

5 medium-sized vine-ripened tomatoes
    (approx. 1½ pounds altogether)
good squeeze of lemon juice
Maldon or other sea salt
handful freshly chopped chervil

Chop the shallot and garlic as finely as is humanly possible—or just blitz to a pulp in a processor—and put in a small bowl with the oil, a pinch of salt and a grinding of pepper, and leave to steep while you blanch the tomatoes: that's to say, put them in a large bowl then pour boiling water over them so that they are hotly submerged. Leave for 5 minutes then tip into a colander and run under cold water. Using a sharp knife, peel off the skins (which is now easy), then cut these fuzzy spheres into slices, as thick or as thin as you like (I like them somewhere in the middle). Arrange the tomatoes in a dish and pour over the dressing, using your fingers to mix well. I find it easier to use one bowl for steeping purposes and another one, later, for serving. You can let the tomatoes sit like this for a good couple of hours. Yes, some liquid will collect, but the flavors will deepen wonderfully.

When you're ready to eat, either leave the dressed tomatoes in the bowl or decant to a new one, but either way, using your hands, turn them to coat, squeeze over some lemon juice, and sprinkle with salt and a tablespoon or so of freshly chopped chervil. Use another herb if you like, but there is one inflexible rule governing this salad: it must be served at room temperature. Leave it in the refrigerator until the last minute and all will be lost.

CHOCOLATE POTS

Despite my antipathy for the ramekin-bound and single-portioned, I make no apology for these. Partly, I suppose, it's nostalgia: when I was a child, these dense, dark, just-solid offerings, known more familiarly then by the French tag *petits pots aux chocolats*, were the dernier cri in bistro chic. Then they were served, as they still are in France, in small white amphora-shaped vessels, small urns with their curved handles, in relief, tilting upward toward the expectant eater. There's nothing to stop you using them now; I would if I weren't so sold on the Polystyrene cups recast in porcelain that you see opposite. The silky chocolate mixture contained within them is just mousse without the whisked egg whites, easier to make and somehow less vulgar, for all the daintiness of their presentation.

The method used to make them is ludicrously simple and done, necessarily, in advance. You just process the lot, pour them into small containers (coffee cups would be fine: there's no need to make a production out of it) and sit them in the refrigerator to set. I stumbled across this method in one of Nick Nairn's books. He, in turn, got it from Hilaire Walden. I've tinkered somewhat with the traditional flavors, adding spices to bring to this the aromatic richness of Mexican hot chocolate (or so I, in my unfounded fantasy, like to think), which tempers the uncompromising richness of the confection without losing its seductive intensity.

6 ounces best-quality bittersweet chocolate, minimum 70% cocoa solids

½ cup plus 2 tablespoons heavy cream

⅓ cup plus 1 tablespoon whole milk

½ teaspoon vanilla extract

½ teaspoon allspice

1 egg

8 ¼-cup pots or custard cups

Crush the chocolate to smithereens in the food processor. Heat the cream and milk until just about boiling, add the vanilla and allspice and pour through the funnel over the chocolate. Let stand for 30 seconds. Process for 30 seconds, then crack the egg down the funnel and process for 45 seconds.

Pour into whatever little cups you're serving in, and sit them in the refrigerator for 6 hours or overnight. But remember to take them out of the refrigerator a good 20 minutes before you want them to be eaten; the chill interferes with their luscious, silky richness.

This makes 2 cups altogether: enough to fill 8 little pots of approximately ¼ cup capacity. But if you've got only bigger cups, just augment quantities.

Aromatic lamb-shank stew with couscous
Crème brûlée

The specification that this is a kitchen supper holds only notional weight: along with most people in the country, I have no dining room. The gracious option is one, then, not open to me. So what I mean here is a dinner party that concentrates on getting friends round the table and feeding them well. There's no starter, the main course is a vast bowlful of unkempt stew; dessert, however elegant, comes in one big dish, to be plonked down and dug into unceremoniously.

AROMATIC LAMB-SHANK STEW

Don't let the word "stew" put you off. Yes, I know it's crippled with connotations of school-dinner gristle and gluey-gravied mess, but the lamb shanks here are anything but that. Of course, you could use shoulder, cut into greed-satisfying chunks, and it still wouldn't be compromise, but the bone in the shank gives such rounded richness of flavor and there's something so unpretentiously satisfying about the great meaty hunkiness of it on the plate. Since supermarkets now routinely stock (or will order in) lamb shanks, and since they're both meaty and cheap, it makes sense to seek them out for this.

The spicing, the muddy softening of the lentils within, owe something to Moroccan cooking, but only obliquely. I've used the seasonings—Marsala wine, soy—I have regularly to hand (unlike restaurant chefs, I don't restock my nonexistent pantry for each new recipe) to bring to this stew the mellow depth I want to find.

As with all stews, this is even better made in advance and reheated; for me, this only makes things easier. The couscous, however, needs to be made last minute. If you don't own a couscoussier (and there's no reason why you should), just steam these grains above boiling water in an ordinary vegetable steamer. Of course it's possible to cook couscous just by steeping it in boiling water (and check package instructions for directions) but I can't honestly tell you it will make the grains as fluffily light.

Otherwise, with this aromatic, sauce-rich stew, just serve plain rice—or a bowlful of buttery mash, of half potatoes, half parsnips, well seasoned and spiced with mace.

6 tablespoons peanut or vegetable oil
8 lamb shanks
2 onions
4 cloves of garlic
sprinkling of salt
1 tablespoon turmeric
1 teaspoon ground ginger
1 dried red chilli pepper, crumbled, or
   ¼ teaspoon dried red pepper flakes
2 teaspoons cinnamon
¼ teaspoon freshly grated nutmeg

black pepper
3 tablespoons honey
1 tablespoon soy sauce
3 tablespoons Marsala wine
6 tablespoons red lentils

to serve:
3 tablespoons chopped pistachios,
   chopped blanched almonds or a
   mixture of both

Put 3 tablespoons of the oil into a very large, wide, heavy-bottomed pan and warm over medium heat. Brown the lamb shanks, in batches, in the pan and then remove to a roasting pan or whatever else you've got at hand to sit them in.

Peel the onions and garlic and process in a food processor or chop them finely by hand. Add the remaining oil to the pan, and fry the onion-garlic mush until soft, sprinkling salt over to stop it sticking.

Stir in the turmeric, ground ginger, chilli, cinnamon and nutmeg, and season with some freshly ground pepper. Stir again, adding the honey, soy sauce and Marsala. Put the shanks back in the pan, add cold water almost to cover, bring to the boil then put a lid on the pan, lower the heat and simmer very gently for 1–1½ hours or until the meat is tender.

Add the red lentils and cook for about 20 minutes longer without the lid, until the lentils have softened into the sauce and the juices have reduced and thickened slightly. Check for seasoning.

Toast the nuts by heating them for a few minutes in a dry frying pan, and sprinkle onto the lamb as you serve it.

Serves 6.

COUSCOUS

The lamb shanks can be cooked in advance: this, as I've said, needs to be done at the last minute. But relax, it's a low-effort undertaking.

About 2¾ cups (18 ounces) couscous
2 teaspoons salt
4 cardamom pods
approx. 2 tablespoons unsalted butter
   in two slices

2 tablespoons sliced almonds
scant ¼ cup pine nuts
2 tablespoons pistachios

Fill the bottom of a steamer, or base of a couscoussier should you possess one, with water and bring to the boil. When it looks like it's almost ready to boil, fill the kettle and put it on, then empty the couscous into a glass bowl, add the salt, crush in the cardamom and mix with your fingers, then pour over a quart of boiling water from the kettle and place a plate on top of the bowl. Leave to stand for 5 minutes, then drain and empty into the steamer or couscoussier top and sit this on top of the boiling water beneath. Add the slices of butter on top of the couscous then clamp on the lid and let steam for 7–10 minutes, by which time the couscous should be tenderly cooked and the butter melting. (You can do this a simpler way if you prefer, by just steeping the couscous in the boiling water for 10–15 minutes, but the grains will be more dense and more likely to clump. It's not disastrous, however, and you must decide what you're prepared to do.)

Meanwhile, toast the almonds by frying them in a dry pan till fragrant and golden, remove them to a plate, then do the same to the pine nuts. Chop the pistachios. Once the couscous is cooked, tip into a bowl, fork through (and always use a fork for mixing or fluffing up couscous; a spoon will crush it and turn it stodgy), sprinkling in the almonds and pine nuts as you do so (and taste for seasoning at the same time, too). Now fork in most of the pistachios, and sprinkle those that remain lightly on top.

CRÈME BRÛLÉE

The first thing you should know about crème brûlée is that it's not hard to make. And few desserts are as voluptuously, seductively easy to eat. I never make mine in little individual ramekins (though there's nothing to stop you if that's what you prefer) but in one large dish: there is something so welcoming about a big bowlful, the rich, smooth, eggy cream waiting to ooze out on the spoon that breaks through the tortoiseshell disk on top.

You don't need me to tell you about the blowtorch bit; this has been rehearsed enough. But it isn't a gimmick or a gratuitous act of showmanship: just the best way of burning the sprinkled-over sugar to instant, brittle compactness. You can get a blowtorch now from more or less any kitchen shop; and there's something curiously satisfying about wielding it.

2½ cups heavy cream	3 generous tablespoons granulated sugar
1 vanilla bean	approx. 6 tablespoons Demerara or
8 egg yolks	granulated brown sugar

Put a pie dish of about 8 inches in diameter in the freezer for at least 20 minutes. Half-fill the sink with cold water. This is just a precaution in case the custard looks as if it's about to split, in which case you should plunge the pan into the water and whisk the custard. I'm not saying it will—with so many egg yolks in the rich cream, it thickens quickly and easily enough—but I always feel better if I've done this.

Put the cream and vanilla bean into a saucepan and bring to the boiling point, but do not let boil. Beat the eggs and sugar together in a bowl, and, still beating, pour the flavored cream over it, bean and all. Rinse and dry the pan and pour the custard mix back in. Cook over medium heat (or low, if you're scared) until the custard thickens, whisking almost constantly: about 10 to 12 minutes should do it. You do want this to be a good, voluptuous crème, so don't err on the side of runny caution. Remember, you've got your sinkful of cold water to plunge the pan into should it really look as if it's about to split.

When the cream's thick enough, take out the vanilla bean, retrieve the pie dish and pour this crème into the severely chilled container. Leave to cool, then put in the refrigerator till truly cold. Sprinkle with Demerara sugar, spoonful by spoonful, and burn with a blowtorch till you have a blistered tortoiseshell covering on top.

Put back in the refrigerator if you want, but remember to take it out a good 20 minutes before serving. At which stage, put the bowl on the table and, with a large spoon and unchecked greed, crack through the sugary carapace and delve into the satin-velvet, vanilla-speckled cream beneath. No more talking: just eat.

NOTES

NOTES

_____

_____

_____

_____

_____

_____

_____

_____

_____

_____

_____

_____

_____

_____

_____

CHAPTER NINE

SLOW-COOK WEEKEND

The point about weekend food is not that you've got more time to cook it, but that you've got more time to eat it. I like to do the sort of cooking that gets on with itself slowly, so that I can potter about the house unencumbered and invite people to lunch without having to slave from first thing in the morning. Most of all, the food shouldn't be about performance and high-strive presentation, but about lingered-over plenty.

SATURDAY LUNCH FOR 6–8

Warm shredded lamb salad with mint and pomegranate
Peppers with feta and almonds
Turkish delight syllabub

This is—give or take—a regular kitchen fallback position for me on Saturdays. It can be streamlined or amplified to suit how I feel and who's coming, but the main thing is that most of the food is prepared either in advance or without strenuous effort. Most times, if it's lunch, I wouldn't go full out with dessert, but just buy huge wedges of two or three cheeses, maybe leaving the feta on the peppers out of the equation, and let people pick their way to a languorous conclusion. And this is the point of this sort of meal: it is about mood, pace, companionship. Why else are you going to be cooking for people?

WARM SHREDDED LAMB SALAD WITH MINT AND POMEGRANATE

The virtue of this is that you can cook the lamb overnight, which means all you need to do is shred the meat, dress it and make the salads at lunchtime itself. Or put it in the oven at a slightly higher temperature, but still unfrenetically low, in the morning and fiddle about as people arrive. You do need to serve the lamb salad warm rather than cold (a bit of fat provides flavorsome lubrication at anything above room temperature; once cold we're talking congealed, waxy whiteness—not such an attractive proposition), but if you keep the lamb tented with foil once it's out of the oven—should you need to hold it for longer than an hour or two—that shouldn't pose problems.

If it's not the pomegranate season you have a choice: either use pomegranate molasses (a tablespoonful or so, diluted with an equal amount of water), which you can get at some supermarkets now, or just use lemon juice and maybe even a little very finely grated zest.

1 shoulder of lamb (approx. 5½ pounds)
4 shallots, halved but not peeled
6 cloves garlic
1 carrot, peeled and halved

Maldon or other sea salt
2¼ cups boiling water
small handful freshly chopped mint
1 pomegranate

Preheat the oven to 250°F.

On the stovetop, brown the lamb, fat-side down, in a large roasting pan. Remove when nicely browned across its middle (you won't get much more than this) and set aside while you fry the vegetables briefly. Just tip them into the pan—you won't need to add any more fat—and cook them, sprinkled with the salt, gently for a couple of minutes. Pour the water over and then replace the lamb, this time fat-side up. Let the liquid in the pan come to a boil, then tent with foil and put in the preheated oven.

Now just leave it there while you sleep. I find that if I put the lamb in before I go to bed, it's perfect by lunchtime the next day. But the point is, at this temperature, nothing's going to go wrong with the lamb if you cook it for a little less or a little more.

If you want to cook the lamb the day you're going to eat it, heat the oven to 325°F and give it 5 hours or so. The point is to find a way of cooking that suits you: you know what sort of pottering relaxes you and what makes you feel constrained; how much time you've got, and how you want to use it. Don't let the food, the kitchen or the imagined expectations of other people bully you.

With that homily over, about an hour before you want to eat, remove the lamb from the pan to a large plate or carving board—not that it needs carving; the deal here is that it's unfashionably overcooked, falling to tender shreds at the touch of a fork. This is the best way to deal with shoulder of lamb: it's cheaper than leg, and the flavor is deeper, better, truer, but even good carvers, which I most definitely am not, can get unstuck trying to slice it.

I get on with the peppers while the lamb's sitting meekly, but you could equally have done this earlier, too (and see the following recipe for instructions). But to finish the lamb salad, simply pull it to pieces with a couple of forks on a large plate. Sprinkle with more sea salt and some freshly chopped mint, then cut the pomegranate in half and dot with the seeds from one of the halves. This is easily done; there's a simple trick, which means you never have to think of winkling out the jeweled pips with a safety pin ever again. Simply hold the pomegranate half above the plate, take a wooden spoon and start bashing the curved skin side with it. Nothing will happen for a few seconds, but have faith. In a short while the glassy red, juicy beads will start raining down.

Take the other half and squeeze the preposterously pink juices over the warm shredded meat. Take to the table and serve.

What I do with the leftovers is warm a pita bread in the microwave, and then spread it with a greedy dollop of hummus, then take the chill off the refrigerated lamb in the microwave (and see earlier notes on cold fat) and stuff the already gooey pita with it. Add freshly chopped mint, black pepper and whatever else you like; raw, finely chopped red onion goes dangerously well.

PEPPERS WITH FETA AND ALMONDS

This is really a vegetarian take on that classic combination of charred, peeled peppers and anchovies. And if it makes little sense in talking about a vegetarian version when this is paired with the lamb salad, then let me reassure you that there is no need to do it all. This pepper and feta combo, with an arugula (or other green) salad, some grilled eggplant dressed, as with the lamb, with pomegranate and mint (or if you're not feeling up to that, just a bowl of good store-bought hummus) and a pile of warmed pita breads, would make the perfect Saturday lunch, vegetarians or no.

8 red or yellow peppers or a mixture of both

4 ounces feta cheese (or 8 ounces if not serving the lamb)

couple of squeezes lemon juice

1 tablespoon extra-virgin olive oil

⅓ cup blanched or sliced almonds

2 tablespoons freshly chopped flat-leaf parsley

Peeling peppers is a time-consuming and fiddly job, but it isn't difficult—and this is a distinction that's important to remember. Like most tasks of this order, culinary or otherwise, the space it takes up in your head is greater than the actual demands of the activity, but if the idea of charring and then peeling eight peppers really appalls, then don't do it. The world is not going to fall apart if you buy a jar of ready-peeled and oil-softened peppers, nor do you lose the right to occupy your own kitchen if you ignore my suggestion altogether. Make a tomato salad; buy some tabbouleh from the deli.

But meanwhile at stately Wayne mansion, preheat the broiler as hot as you can get it, and then sit the peppers on a rack below. When the skin turns black and blistery, turn them; you want to char them on every side. You can do this also, if you've got a gas stove, just by holding them with a long fork over the burner, but it can get tiresome to say the least.

When the peppers are black and charred, remove them (trying not to burn yourself) to a large bowl and cover immediately with plastic wrap. Leave for 10–20 minutes.

Then uncover and, one by one, peel and seed the peppers. Don't get worried if the odd bit of skin (or indeed seed) remains. Cut or tear into wide chunks/strips (I don't like this too dinky) and arrange on a large plate. Crumble over the feta, then squeeze over lemon juice and drizzle with oil. Scatter over the almonds and sprinkle on the parsley— and that, frankly, is it.

Leftovers can be stuffed into pita breads, as with the lamb, but the sweet, salty mix is also lovely as a sauce for pasta (better without the almonds, though I'd bet they'd all be picked off anyway by the time you got to leftover stage). Cook some penne, reserve a coffee cupful of the cooking water on draining, then toss the pasta back into the hot pan with half the reserved water and a small bowlful of peppers and feta. Toss around so that everything begins to cohere (but not actually cook) and turn into a bowl. Eat.

TURKISH DELIGHT SYLLABUB

This hasn't got the temple-aching sweetness of Turkish Delight, nor its palate-cleaving glutinousness, but rather it is a cloud-light spoon-pudding version that attempts to catch its aromatic essence—perfect after the lamb and pomegranate salad. That it requires no cooking, merely some pouring and whisking, doesn't hurt either.

I use Cointreau here, simply because I have an enormous bottle of it and I prefer not to have to whip out to the shops every time I want to make something, but if you've got any other drink that you feel would make a suitable base, then feel free to use it in its stead. The quantities here make enough syllabub to fill, billowingly, eight 5-ounce glasses.

³/₄ cup Cointreau
juice of 2 lemons
8 tablespoons sugar
just under 2¹/₂ cups heavy cream

2 tablespoons rosewater
2 tablespoons orangeflower water
2 tablespoons shelled pistachios, finely
  chopped

Combine the Cointreau, lemon juice and sugar in a large bowl (I use the bowl of my KitchenAid mixer) and stir to dissolve the sugar, or as good as. Slowly stir in the cream then get whisking. As I said, I use my freestanding mixer for this, but if you haven't got one, don't worry—but I would then advise a handheld electric mixer. This takes *ages* to thicken and doing it by hand will drive you demented with tedium and impatience. Or it would me.

When the cream's fairly thick, but still not thick enough to hold its shape, dribble in the flower waters and then keep whisking until you have a creamy mixture that's light and airy but able to form soft peaks. I always think of syllabub as occupying some notional territory between solid and liquid; you're aiming, as you whisk, for what food writer Jane Grigson called "bulky whiteness." Whatever: better slightly too runny than slightly too thick, so proceed carefully, but don't get anxious about it. You can anyway probably see the texture it is from the picture, opposite.

Spoon the syllabub in airy dollops into small glasses, letting the mixture billow up above the rim of the glass, and scatter finely chopped pistachios on top. In my book *How to Eat*, there's a recipe for pistachio crescents that would be fabulous dunked into and eaten with this. But only if you feel like it: the cool, fool-like smoothness of this is perfect as it is.

SUNDAY LUNCH FOR 12

**Slow-roasted aromatic shoulder of pork with creamy potato gratin
and stir-braised Savoy cabbage with nigella seeds
Easy sticky-toffee pudding**

You are just going to have to believe me when I tell you that there is such a thing as a lazy Sunday lunch for twelve and, keep calm, I propose you cook it. The reason you should believe me is that I am not someone who churns out vats of food without the merest furrowing of a brow or clenching of a knuckle. True, I like cooking, and I like my friends, but having to feed too many of them in my kitchen at one time can turn me into someone positively curdled with resentment and panic. I'd like to be calm, I'd like to be unflappable, but some things are just never going to come to pass.

So, working along the premise of change what you can and accept what you can't, I've found a way of cooking that satisfies my need to be hospitable while accommodating my hostessly shortcomings. The first imperative is that there should be a great deal, indeed too much, to eat. It might sound blasphemous to say that my Jewish-mother leanings are best satisfied by the roasting of a whole shoulder of pork, but I'm afraid I've found this to be the case. The fact that this great weight of pig needs hardly any interference from you while it cooks satisfies the second requirement, namely that you are not working yourself up into a lather during the little free time you might have. But it's not quite as unsatisfying as that sounds: before you put the pork into the oven (where you leave it for a full day) you smother it with a fragrant paste of your own making, thereby giving yourself some essential element of kitchen pottering, without which you may as well be pinging the microwave, psychologically speaking.

Without wishing to sound like Marie Antoinette, I do feel that pork does have to be the very best pork to start off with, not bred to flabby leanness in some godforsaken pig penitentiary. These days this can be harder to find than it sounds. I suggest you seek out organic, naturally grown pork. I'm not suggesting you spend more than you can, but with meat particularly—as we've learned, or are beginning to learn, surely—it's better to buy the best occasionally, than the disreputably cut-price often. And don't necessarily disdain your local butcher, if you're lucky enough to have one still; indeed, if you don't go to your butcher ever, there soon won't be any left to go to.

Once, with my order, my supplier sent me a photo of "the girls" on a grassy hill overlooking Lyme Bay, which I stuck on my refrigerator. And although I realize it might sound macabre to some of you to be gazing at a picture of live pigs while cooking a dead one, I actually think it a whole lot healthier than buying sanitized packages of plastic-wrapped meat from the supermarket that pretends to have no relationship with its source. Tastes a whole lot better, too.

The paste I spread on this pork is made of ginger, garlic, chilli and sherry vinegar, which has a Chinesey tone to it. Indeed, the pork when it's finished—the crackling glazed and crisp, the flesh beneath melting and to be torn rather than carved—reminds me obscurely of Peking duck. There's the same mixture of velvet-tender meat and seared-crisp skin.

SLOW-ROASTED AROMATIC SHOULDER OF PORK

I first got the idea of cooking a shoulder of pork over 24 hours like this from the second *River Café Cookbook*; my take on it is really a de-Italianized version. Any mixture of herbs or spices you want would do: this isn't a recipe so much as a suggestion.

1 shoulder of pork, skin scored (approx. 12–14 pounds)	**2 fresh red chillies or 1 teaspoon dried red pepper flakes**
6 garlic cloves	**3 tablespoons olive oil (not extra-virgin)**
½-inch length of fresh ginger	**4 tablespoons sherry or rice vinegar**

The pork takes 24 hours to cook, which is no cause for alarm, because for about 23 hours and 55 minutes you are ignoring it absolutely. And it makes your house smell like a home should.

So, if you're planning to eat this for Sunday lunch, at about Saturday lunchtime, preheat your (clean) oven to the hottest it will go. Sit the pork skin-side up on a rack over a roasting pan. I like to use a mortar and pestle to make my paste because it makes me feel good, but you could just grate the garlic and ginger (one of my beloved, and often mentioned, Microplane graters is the tool for the job) and stir in chilli flakes, a tablespoonful of oil and two of vinegar if you want. Otherwise, pound together the peeled chopped ginger and peeled cloves with the fresh chilli, adding a tablespoonful of oil and two of vinegar when they're squished and pastelike.

Using your fingers, rub this paste over the scored skin, pushing bits into the cut lines of rind. Stagger across to the oven and put in the tray, leaving it for 30 minutes. Meanwhile, into the bowl in which you mixed the paste, pour the two remaining tablespoons each of oil and vinegar. When the pork's had its half an hour, remove it from the oven, turning it to 225°F as you do so. Now turn the pork over: I find it easiest to lift it by hand wearing oven mitts. It makes them dirty, OK, but there is the washing machine. . . .

Pour the oil and vinegar over the underside (which is now uppermost on the rack) and put the pork back in the low oven, leaving it there for 23 hours. (Actually, you could leave it longer. One of the joys of this is that it cannot overcook.) Anyway, after 23 hours, or 30–40 minutes before you actually want to eat, turn the oven back to the highest it will go, remove the pork and turn it back crackling-side up. Put it back in the oven for 30 minutes, in which time it will get hot and crisp, though you can give it another 10 if you feel it needs it.

Remove, slice off the crackling in a horizontal swipe of the knife and break it into manageable pieces, then start carving or pulling at the tender meat.

CREAMY POTATO GRATIN

My not entirely orthodox way of turning out this otherwise classic dish of cream-softened potatoes has a lot going for it here. The thing is, you cook the potatoes first in a pan in the stove, which means that, one, you can do it in advance up to the final and quick blast in the oven (always a boon for me); two, you don't therefore need a double oven, because you blitz the potatoes while the pork's having its post-roasting rest; and, three, this is the best way of making sure the potatoes are actually cooked to margin blurring softness there is nothing worse than biting into a potato gratin that bites back.

4½ pounds all-purpose potatoes

2 cups whole milk

2 cups heavy cream

1 onion, peeled

2 cloves garlic, minced

1 tablespoon salt

approx. ¼ cup unsalted butter

Preheat the oven to 500°F.

Peel the potatoes and cut them into slices, neither especially thin nor especially thick (approximately ½ inch) and put them into a large saucepan with the milk, cream, onion, minced garlic and salt. Bring to the boil and cook at a robust simmer or gentle boil (however you like to think of it) until verging on tender, but not dissolving into mush. The pan might be hell to clean afterward, but any excuse for long, lazy soaking rather than brisk pre- or postprandial scrubbing always appeals to me. And, for what it's worth, I find that when pans are really, dauntingly, stuck with cooked-on gunge, it's more effective to soak them in hot water and detergent (i.e., the stuff you put in the washing machine, though I haven't tried, and don't think I would, with tablets) rather than dish liquid.

Use some of the butter to grease a large roasting pan (15 x 12 inches) and then pour the almost sludgy milk and potato mixture into it. Dot with remaining butter and cook in the oven for 15 minutes or until the potato is bubbly and browned on top. Remove, let stand for 10–20 minutes and then serve.

This is not the most laborsaving way of cooking potatoes, to be sure, but one of the most seductive. And it reheats well as an accompaniment to cold roast pork, or indeed anything, in the days that follow.

STIR-BRAISED SAVOY CABBAGE WITH NIGELLA SEEDS

Forgive the culinary egomania, not meant entirely seriously you do understand, but I bought a tin of nigella seeds in Dean & Deluca, the world's most pulse-quickening food shop, when I was in New York once, and I can't just let it sit in the cupboard unused—forever. Actually, this spice is no impossible-to-find delicacy: it's a regular in Indian food, and can be found labeled "kalonji," in a variety of spellings, or sometimes "black cumin" or "black onion seeds" in far-from-recherché outlets. Don't think twice, though, about substituting ordinary cumin seeds.

1 large Savoy cabbage or two smaller   Maldon or other sea salt to taste
3 tablespoons vegetable oil   few drops soy sauce
1 tablespoon nigella seeds   few drops toasted sesame oil
2 cups vegetable stock

Halve the cabbage or cabbages, cut out the core and finely shred it.

Warm the oil in a wide but deep saucepan that has a lid, and patiently toss the cabbage in the oil over a low to medium heat until it's evenly but finely glossed and beginning to wilt. Sprinkle in the nigella seeds and turn well so that they are evenly distributed. Pour in the stock, toss the cabbage again, salt well or cautiously depending on how salty the stock is, and clamp on the lid, leaving the cabbage to steam for 4 minutes or so. Remove the lid and taste to see how cooked the cabbage is. I find that 4 minutes more or less does it for me, by which time I give the cabbage another minute, while stirring, with the lid off. Splash with soy and sesame oil, toss again and transfer to a warmed bowl or bowls.

EASY STICKY-TOFFEE DESSERT

This draws on the culinary technology of the surprise dessert—that amazing affair by which, on baking, a layer of cake is formed, under which evolves a thick and luscious sauce—while playing with the flavors of a traditional sticky-toffee pudding. True, if you're feeding 12 people you'll need to make two, but given how almost provocatively easy it is, that's no big deal. I can see this stretching to 8, maybe even a little bit beyond, but I wouldn't want to ask much more of it, despite the gargantuan feast that precedes it. Better to have too much than give rise to even the slightest tremor of ration-anxiety at the table. Never Knowingly Undercatered, that's me.

for the cake:
scant 1/3 cup dark brown sugar, packed
1 cup plus 2 tablespoons self-rising flour
1/2 cup whole milk
1 egg
1 teaspoon vanilla extract
1/4 cup unsalted butter, melted
3/4 cup plus 2 tablespoons chopped,
  rolled dates

for the sauce:
3/4 cup dark brown sugar, packed
approx. 2 tablespoons unsalted butter in
  little blobs
2 1/4 cups boiling water

Preheat the oven to 375°F and butter a 1 1/2-quart capacity baking dish.

Combine the sugar with the flour in a large bowl. Pour the milk into a measuring cup, beat in the egg, vanilla and melted butter and then pour this mixture over the sugar and flour, stirring—just with a wooden spoon—to combine. Fold in the dates then scrape into the prepared baking dish. Don't worry if it doesn't look very full: it will do by the time it cooks.

Sprinkle over the sugar for the sauce and dot with the butter. Pour over the boiling water (yes really!) and transfer to the oven. Set the timer for 45 minutes, though you might find the dessert needs 5 or 10 minutes more. The top of the dessert should be springy and spongy when it's cooked; underneath, the butter, dark brown sugar and boiling water will have turned into a rich, sticky sauce. Serve with vanilla ice cream, crème fraîche or heavy or light cream as you wish.

Serves 6–8.

NOTES

CHAPTER TEN

TEMPLEFOOD

I think I'd better start by explaining what Templefood is: it's my term for the soothing, pure, would-be restorative food I make for myself after one binge or late night too many. "Temple" as in "my body is a. . . ."

Well, mine's not, but this is what I eat when I want to feel it is. And don't think—as if—I'm counseling deprivation or restraint, but rather the holy glow of self-indulgently virtuous pleasure. . . .

PRAIRIE OYSTER

How much pleasure you could get out of this I'm not sure, but it's a preliminary rather than regular feature of the restoration process. My templefood times tend to start with, indeed are prompted by, a hangover and so I thought it made sense to start this chapter with a hangover cure. Working on Nietzsche's principle that what doesn't kill you makes you stronger, I won't make any apologies for the daunting concoction that follows. The point is, if you can survive this, you can survive anything.

There's no oyster involved, but the name from this drink comes, I suspect, from the slang term used by ranchers for a bull's testicle, which the egg yolk suspended in the alcohol was thought to resemble—and which I'm sure makes you all feel very much better.

1 egg yolk	**couple of dashes Tabasco**
3 tablespoons brandy	**a few drops Worcestershire sauce**
a few drops malt vinegar	**salt and pepper**

Put the egg yolk in a margarita glass. Mix the remaining ingredients and pour over yolk. Gulp down in one.

Serves 1.

Note: Consuming raw eggs can cause salmonella. Check the quality of the eggs in your area to see if salmonella is a problem, and do not consume if you are pregnant or have a chronic illness or compromised immune system.

SALMON WITH GREENS AND SHIITAKE MUSHROOMS

My templefood days do not consist of fey picking: this is gratifyingly substantial. In order to enjoy it you don't have to know that salmon is rich in omega-3 oils, which are beneficial, indeed essential, to good health, and that shiitake mushrooms are believed, by the Japanese at least, to contain cancer-fighting properties, but it all helps in the aim of wallowing in virtuous well-being.

But the most important thing I can tell you is that this is *good*.

2 skinned salmon fillets, preferably organic
1 clove garlic, finely minced or chopped
2 tablespoons vegetable or peanut oil
generous ¹/₂ cup shiitake mushrooms, stemmed and sliced

14 ounces (about 1³/₄ cups) bok choy sum or bok choy, roughly chopped, with stalks separated from leaves
3 tablespoons soy sauce
1 teaspoon sesame oil
pepper to taste

Cook the salmon fillets—preferably in a good nonstick pan or on a griddle—over medium-high heat until just cooked through, and remove them to warmed plates while you get on with or finish the vegetables (you can start them off as the salmon cooks).

In a heavy-based pan, fry the garlic in the oil until it is warm but not sticking. Add the sliced mushrooms together with the bok choy sum stalks, stirring everything together for a bare minute or so. Cover the pan and cook for about 5 minutes, remove the lid and add the roughly chopped bok choy sum leaves, soy sauce and sesame oil, then let it cook for another 2–3 minutes until the leaves have wilted.

Pile the mushrooms and greens on the plates with the salmon, add pepper to taste and, pleasurably, eat. I sometimes make a little sauce to go with, by mixing Colman's mustard powder into a smooth paste with a little cold water, adding a few drops of soy sauce and (a Microplane grater makes easy work of this) a scant, pulpy purée of fresh ginger.

Serves 2.

GINGERY-HOT DUCK SALAD

I don't buy into this anti-meat drive. Indeed, I am vehemently pro-protein. Nor am I fat-phobic, so I tend to leave the fatty layer of skin on the duck breast before I grill (or fry) it, but remove it before cooking by all means if you have succumbed to the lure of the lean. And if that's the case, you'll be pleased to learn that not one drop of oil need go into the dressing. However, I often sprinkle a little toasted sesame oil over at the end, which is why I've still listed it in the ingredients. Your call.

The salad itself is a slight reworking of a Cambodian beef salad I often make; here the lime juice in the steeping mixture (which turns into the dressing) is supplemented with orange juice (Asian evocations of duck à l'orange and all that), but in season, around January, use instead of this combination the fragrantly acerbic juice of one Seville orange.

1 duck breast
2 tablespoons fish sauce (nam pla)
juice of ½ lime and juice of ½ orange,
  or of 1 Seville orange
1 small red chilli, finely chopped

½-inch piece of fresh ginger, grated
few drops sesame oil (optional)
2 ounces (about ¼ cup) baby spinach,
  watercress, lamb's lettuce or a mixture

Grill or sauté the duck breast—fat-side down if not removed—for 10 to 12 minutes or until it's cooked to juicy pinkness.

Let it rest on a board while you mix the fish sauce, lime and orange juice (or just Seville-orange juice), chilli, ginger and optional sesame oil together in a bowl.

Pour any juices that the duck has made into the bowl, and then carve the meat on the diagonal into thin slices. Toss the sliced duck into the bowl and stir everything well. Turn it out onto a serving plate covered with the salad leaves.

Serves 2.

HOT AND SOUR SOUP

I know that for some people nothing feels more restoring than something warm and unchallengingly bland, but when it's succor and sustenance I need, it's spice that I want. This soup, tom yam—the culinary equivalent of Friar's Balsam—clears the tubes and brings fire to the jaded soul. And there's nothing like a bit of searing heat to push away any hungover seediness. It's good for those days when you're thick with cold, too.

It's easy to throw together: the chicken stock I make out of boiling water and bouillon granules, and the tom yam hot and sour paste is sold now at most supermarkets, along with the other ingredients, too.

6½ cups chicken stock

1 heaping tablespoon tom yam hot and sour paste

4 kaffir lime leaves, finely chopped, optional

1 stick lemongrass, tender inner part only, roughly chopped

juice of 1 lime

4 tablespoons fish sauce (nam pla)

2–3 small jalapeños or fresh red or green chillies, finely chopped

1 teaspoon sugar

1½ cups plus 2 tablespoons straw or button mushrooms, halved or quartered according to size

1 pound 2 ounces peeled raw shrimp, thawed if frozen

5 small scallions, cut into short lengths and then into strips

small bunch cilantro, chopped

Heat the stock and tom yam paste in a decent-sized saucepan with the lime leaves, lemongrass, lime juice, fish sauce, chillies and sugar. Bring to the boil, add the mushrooms and simmer for a couple of minutes, then add the shrimp and scallions and cook for a further 2–3 minutes, or until the shrimp are cooked but still tender. Sprinkle with a little cilantro and put more on the table for people to add themselves as they want.

Serves 4–6.

VIETNAMESE CHICKEN AND MINT SALAD

This is what I make when a temple-mooded girlfriend or two are coming over not so much for dinner as to talk or moan, as one does, during those chapter meetings of the martyred sisterhood. It's very quick as long as you've got a food processor (and not that time-consuming without) and ideal for picking at with an outstretched fork over a drawn-out evening. The dressing needs to steep for half an hour, but you don't need to do anything to it while it's going on.

This recipe is adapted from *The Best of Nicole Routhier* and is, or so she explains, the Vietnamese equivalent of coleslaw, but this doesn't quite sum up its fresh appeal and ability to spruce up a girl's flagging spirits. This is a real reviver.

Since it's easy to buy chicken breast ready-cooked, that's what I generally use, but obviously if you've got a leftover chicken in the refrigerator I suggest you use that. Likewise, consider using the baby cabbages you see around these days: they are exactly the size you need and easier than hacking away at a big bruiser. All the less familiar ingredients can, as ever, be bought at a supermarket. And by all means leave out the oil in the dressing if including it would make you feel less than virtuous.

This makes a lot, but I find it's very easy to get through—and it stays in the refrigerator for a day or two to provide instant midnight pickings of a not-too-injurious sort.

1 chilli, preferably a hot Thai one, seeded and minced

1 fat garlic clove, peeled and minced

1 tablespoon sugar

1½ teaspoons rice vinegar

1½ tablespoons lime juice

1½ tablespoons Vietnamese or Thai fish sauce (nuoc nam or nam pla)

1½ tablespoons vegetable oil

half a medium onion, finely sliced

black pepper

7–8 ounces white cabbage, shredded

1 medium carrot, shredded, julienned or grated

7 ounces (almost 1 cup) cooked chicken breast, shredded or cut into fine strips

fat bunch of mint, about 3 tablespoons, plus more for garnish

In a bowl, combine the chilli, garlic, sugar, vinegar, lime juice, fish sauce, oil, onion and black pepper to taste. Put to one side for half an hour. Then in a big plate or bowl, mix the cabbage, carrot, chicken and mint. Pour over the onion-soused, chilli-flecked dressing and toss very well—slowly and patiently—so that everything is combined and covered thinly. Taste to see if you need salt or pepper. Serve on a flat plate with maybe a bit more mint chopped on top.

Serves 2–4.

PEACHES AND BLUEBERRIES

Dessert is hardly a feature of the templefood way but, as a girlfriend said to me once, you need to know there's something to stave off that moment of desolation that threatens to settle when eating's done for the day. Hence this: which is frankly not so much a recipe as a suggestion. The colors themselves induce great good mood and, allegedly, blueberries aid memory, though I forget now where I read this.

Mostly I eat this cold, the peaches sliced, the blueberries tumbled over them and a few drops of orangeflower water sprinkled on top, but you can—and this is excellent for breakfast, or when you desperately need the comfort of something hot—just dollop some plain yogurt (0% fat or otherwise) over the roughly assembled fruit, sprinkle the sparsest bit of Demerara sugar on top and then cook in a hottish oven for about 20 minutes—until the fruit's softened and the sugar faintly caramelized. It makes sense particularly to go for the hot option with the leftovers of the first, fresh fruit salad.

These amounts should fill an ovenproof dish measuring approximately 12 x 8 inches.

6 peaches
1½ pints blueberries

1–2 teaspoons orangeflower water

It's difficult to say how many this would serve: it would do 8 definitely, but if it helps to have a stash of ready-made cut-up fruit on hand, then don't feel you need to cut down on quantities for even two of you.

For those days when a yielding peach is hard to find—and there are many of them—my other standby is a papaya halved avocado-style, the seeds removed, a tumble of raspberries tossed into the now-empty cavity and a reviving, flavor-sprucing shot of lime juice squeezed on top.

NOTES

NOTES

_____

_____

_____

_____

_____

_____

_____

_____

_____

_____

_____

_____

_____

_____

_____